T0314867

The Hijab

The Hijab

Islam, Women and the
Politics of Clothing

Edited by

P.K. YASSER ARAFATH
G. ARUNIMA

**SIMON &
SCHUSTER**

London · New York · Sydney · Toronto · New Delhi

First published in India by Simon & Schuster India, 2022
Copyright © Simon & Schuster India, 2022

1 3 5 7 9 10 8 6 4 2

Simon & Schuster India
818, Indraprakash Building,
21, Barakhamba Road,
New Delhi 110001.

www.simonandschuster.co.in

Hardback ISBN: 978-93-92099-38-0
Ebook ISBN: 978-93-92099-32-8

Typeset in India by SÜRYA, New Delhi
Printed and bound in India by Replika Press Pvt. Ltd.

Our inspiration: the Muslim girls and women
protesting for their rights in India and Iran.
This book is dedicated to them.

CONTENTS

PART FOUR: MANY FEMINISMS

PART FIVE: STORY

INTRODUCTION

BANNING THE HIJAB
Politics and Perspectives

P.K. Yasser Arafath and G. Arunima

It's only very recently that wearing the hijab has become controversial in India. While at the moment this is restricted to some educational institutions, mainly schools and pre-university colleges, the fallout of this can be far reaching. While much of the discussions of the hijab ban in India has centred on whether wearing the hijab to school violates the dress code, and the impact of the ban on their education, in other parts of the world where similar bans were invoked earlier, like France, the debate's focus has been on a reappraisal of secularism.

The trigger for the ban on wearing the hijab started with a government run pre-university college in the southern Indian state of Karnataka disallowing Muslim girls from wearing it. The grounds were that it violated the "uniform" or the prescribed dress code in their college. This decision by the school authorities was met with protests by school and pre-university girl students, and those organized by Muslim organisations like the Campus Front of India, without much luck, resulting in their turning to the courts with the hope of a possible reversal of the ban. The Karnataka High Court however upheld the right of the schools to endorse the state government's ban, refuting all the main grounds that had been raised by the students. These included arguing for the right to freedom of conscience (Article 25 in the Indian Constitution) and the right to freedom of expression and privacy.[1] The court dismissed the former contention on the grounds that wearing the hijab wasn't 'an essential practice in Islam.' With regard to the latter the court maintained that the dress code was a "reasonable restriction" and was "religion-neutral" and "universally applicable." The judges added that the dress code promoted 'the principles of secularism.' Though the students have appealed the High Court judgement on grounds that the ban was affecting their studies, arguing that wearing the hijab was essential to their observance and practice, and that it did not 'harm anyone else,' the Supreme Court is yet to begin even preliminary hearings on the matter.[2] While the legal turn in this instance has meant that the terms of reference for the question of Muslim girls' right to wear the hijab to school is now determined by law, the ban and the Karnataka High Court verdict forefronts several issues including the meaning of secularism in such an instance, the rights of Muslim women over their bodies and beliefs, and ways of understanding the hijab itself.

Since hijab banning isn't unique to India, and has

---

1. https://www.scobserver.in/reports/hijab-ban-judgment-summary-karnataka-hc/

2. https://www.thehindu.com/news/national/hijab-row-petitions-filed-by-students-in-limbo-in-supreme-court/article65542379.ece

provoked intense debates and discussions in many parts of the West, it is useful to engage some of the main issues raised in those contexts. In one of the most significant discussions on this issue, feminist historian of France Joan Scott in her work, *Politics of the Veil*, asks why the headscarf became "intolerable" and "controversial" in France?[3] She argues that 'assimilation [was] the only way for Muslims to become French,'[4] for which the pre-condition was making Muslim women remove the hijab from public spaces such as schools. This, the French state argued, was central to the French notion of laicite [secularism], which involved no display of religious affiliation in public. However, this was further qualified by the argument that this pertained specifically to religious objects that were large. The hijab was one such object. The process of translation added a further layer of meaning that was utilized to vilify Islam as a patriarchal religion. As Scott argues, this "conflation" of words involved the hijab, the term used by Muslims in France, to be translated as foulard in French, and in English as the headscarf. Soon the media transformed this into the "veil" (voile) 'with the assumption that the face and body of the wearer is hidden from public.'[5] This is then absorbed quite seamlessly into a narrative about gender equality and its absence in Islam.

In her later work, a wide ranging meditation on the theme of secularism in the west, including its many meanings, Joan Scott unpacks these histories to point out that gender equality wasn't intrinsic to secularism as is

---

3. Scott, Joan Wallach, 2007. *The Politics of the Veil*, 3, Princeton University Press.

4. Ibid., 8.

5. Ibid., 16.

assumed at present.[6] As she argues, '[I]n this discourse secularism guarantees freedom and gender equality while Islam is synonymous with oppression.'[7] In other words, secularism is associated with 'reason, freedom and women's rights' while Islam is seen as a 'culture of oppression and terror.'[8] Historically in France, the separation of church and state meant that religion was relegated to the private sphere, and as Scott's detailed and nuanced work shows secularist campaigns of the nineteenth century 'deployed the language of sex difference in order to disarm the power of religious institutions, not by abolishing those institutions but by feminizing them.'[9] The relegation of religion to the "private sphere," along with women, home, family and affective relationships was to set it aside from the real world of men—state, markets and politics. In fact, as she shows, the only time that French politicians (men) begin to espouse ideas about gender equality is well into the 20th century, and this was mainly in order to contrast French secularism with Islam.

While Joan Scott's argument is a detailed historical exposition of the meanings, and limitations, of secularism she is not alone in critiquing the idea of the secular. Political anthropologist Saba Mahmood's critique of secularism in this context has been powerful and influential. She explores the contradictions of secularism further when she poses the question of whether the principle of freedom to practice

---

6. Scott, Joan Wallach, 2018. *Sex and Secularism*, Princeton University Press.

7. Ibid., 1.

8. Ibid.

9. Ibid., 13.

religion was integral to liberal democracies.[10] In other words, she asks if the secular state is religiously neutral? She poses this question apropos the French banning of the hijab in schools, using the argument that religious symbols cannot be displayed in public in a secular state. For Mahmood, this is an example of secularism's "liberal anxiety"[11] and she asks whether the meaning of secularism was removing religiosity from the public domain, and if the claim that secularism was the 'most effective political solution' to stopping religious conflict was indeed correct.[12] She argues that religion is never really removed from the public domain but 'reshapes the form it takes, the subjectivities it endorses, and the epistemological claims it can make.' She draws on Talal Asad's insight in his important work, *Formations of the Secular*, to demonstrate that the way to understand the secular liberal state's regulation of religious life should be understood 'not as an exception to the norm of liberal rule, but as an exception in the Schmittian sense'[13]—in other words 'as an exercise of sovereign power.' The argument here is that it is the secular state that can authorize certain forms of religious life, practices and subjectivities, and never the other way round. So despite the supposed separation of religion and state, in actual fact this is never the case. "Liberal understanding," she argues, is that religion is simply a system of signs and symbols. So even though many believing Muslim women may see the veil at as a 'means and end to realizing god's will,' liberals usually dismiss it as

---

10. Mahmood, Saba, 2006. 'Secularism, Hermeneutics and Empire: the Politics of Islamic Reformation', *Public Culture*, 18:2, 323-347.

11. Ibid., 326.

12. Ibid.

13. Ibid., 327.

"false consciousness." In other words an "ethical political conception" such as wearing the hijab isn't accorded the meaning that it ought to have, but is seen, at best as signifying women's intentions, or a way to understand the context in which it is adopted.[14]

What is distinctive about the Indian case is that secularism here does not simply mean a separation of religion and state or a removal of the former from public life. While constitutional provisions that define Indian secularism assert that India will not have a state religion, provide religious instruction in schools, or support any religion through state taxes, the right to religion too is protected by the Constitution, including the right to believe, practice and propagate it. In other words, in India religion is not relegated to the private sphere. That said, as Partha Chatterjee demonstrates 'the state has become entangled in the affairs of religion in numerous ways,'[15] including state governments like Tamil Nadu and Kerala paying certain sums of money to the Devaswom funds.[16] This "entanglement" aside, in India one also needs to examine the historical creation of "personal laws." These laws were a colonial invention that clubbed together matters pertaining to family, marriage, property and inheritance together, terming these as "personal," and making these subject to religious laws and interpretation. While a detailed discussion of the history of evolution or transformation of personal laws isn't within the purview of this volume, suffice it to say here that the colonial administration, in its bid to

---

14. Ibid., 343.

15. Chatterjee, Partha, 1998. 'Secularism and Tolerance', in Rajeev Bhargava edited, *Secularism and its Critics*, Oxford University Press, 364.

16. Ibid.

appear non-invasive, relegated personal laws to the realm of religion. This meant that all matters pertaining to those areas defined as "personal" were now to be determined by taking recourse to religious texts, and authority. While this did not result in an instantaneous transformation of these matters, in many cases older, more flexible, customary practices were eroded after having been brought within the ambit of religiously inspired legal interpretation. That said, it is worth mentioning that in the postcolonial context, constitutionally defined Indian secularism permits several different kinds of "personal laws," and customary practices, to co-exist with civil and criminal laws of the country. "Personal" here is religious, and not "private" or feminized as has been the case in France; it is precisely this that guarantees personal laws some protection from state interference. Therefore, despite the ambiguous status of many of these personal laws, the general understanding is that communities should be left to reform, or jettison, any or all of these. This also means that any practice that can be seen as coming under the jurisdiction of "personal laws" can continue undisturbed until these are challenged by members of the community itself. However, in more recent times in India, we see that this is not necessarily the case and there are attempts to erode the status of "personal laws," particularly those based on Islamic jurisprudence.

It is clear from the above discussion that Mahmood's important argument, centred as it is on the French model of secularism and post 9/11 discussions regarding Islam in the US, cannot be applied without qualifications, for an understanding of Indian secularism and its crisis. Indeed the distinction that women's and religious studies scholar Leila Ahmed makes, between "lay" and "establishment" Islam may be more helpful for an understanding of religion per se. She argues that while there is an "ethical impulse" in a lay understanding of Islam, "establishment Islam" is far more invested in political power, and therefore wishes to 'eliminate those who challenge its authority.'[17] This, if transposed to the Indian context, could be said to be true of Hinduism too, where historically popular practices have been ethical, and egalitarian, in spirit (for instance bhakti, or the many subaltern faith practices that have proliferated in the country) whereas "establishment Hinduism" (like Hindutva) is entrenched in political power. Ahmed's was amongst the earliest discussions that located the idea of 'women's oppression in Islamic societies' within a colonial, and racist, discourse inaugurated by the Victorians. As she demonstrates colonizers, despite dismissing feminism's claims locally, utilized its language within their colonial project. She shows the shifts in attitudes regarding education, marriage, family and dress amongst Egyptian women over a century long period, and argues against the simplistic correlation equating forms of dressing in Muslim majority countries with women's oppression. On the contrary, she shows the many reasons for its adoption in the context of the 20th century, including the practical solutions and ease it provides for women, often from rural or lower middle class families, for seeking education, mobility, employment and even the desire to fraternize with men.

This is what makes Emma Tarlo's argument important, as she moves away from querying the meaning of the hijab to asking what it does to the women wearing it.[18]

---

17. Ahmed, Leila, 1992. *Women and Gender in Islam: Historical Roots of a Modern Debate*, Yale University Press.

18. Tarlo, Emma, 2007. 'Hijab in London: Metamorphosis, Resonance and Effects', *Journal of Material Culture*, 1-26.

In other words, she places women's sense of self, and their subjectivity, at the centre while posing questions about their choice to wear the hijab. Such an argument is both about women's sartorial practices, as it is about ocularity. How must one understand the public "visibility" of the hijab wearing woman—an issue that gains relevance when many of the critics of the hijab claim that wearing it is oppressive and makes women "invisible." On the contrary, as Tarlo shows, the hijab wearing woman is visible as both Muslim and woman, thereby posing a serious question about ways of seeing, and the politics of ocularity in contemporary London. In her embedded ethnography, the reasons for wearing the hijab aren't located in explanations that use ethnicity or religion to understand sartorial practices, but are read as much as resistance, or ways of challenging everyday forms of patriarchy. Like Ahmed, Tarlo's work also opens up the possibility of reading the sartorial choice of wearing a hijab as one that is linked to Muslim women's ability to make considered choices and is not necessarily linked to patriarchal or religious enforcement.

Hijab and its History

'In 1959, Mr. G. S. Sagar, a Sikh, applied for a position as a bus conductor with Manchester Transport. His application was rejected because he insisted that he wanted to wear his turban rather than the uniform cap prescribed by the municipality for all its transport workers. Sagar argued that the wearing of the turban was an essential part of his religious beliefs. He didn't understand why, if thousands of Sikhs who had fought and died for the empire in the two World Wars could wear their turbans, he couldn't do so. The transport authorities argued that if an exception to the rules of wearing the proper uniform were allowed there was no telling where the process would end. The uniform could only be maintained if there were no exceptions.'[19] According to Bernard S. Cohn, the whole turban dispute emanated from the white English working-class's xenophobic dislike for the dark-skinned and cheaper Indian labour force which migrated into former colonialist countries and the British people's attitude towards their white-skinned rulers who controlled their dark-skinned subjects across the colonies for centuries.

In a similar way and for similar reasons, European orientalists attempted to fixate vestimentary systems in their colonies two centuries ago with the emergence of pervasive orientalism and colonial modernity. Muslim women who wore clothes that were identified sartorially as Islamic were specifically targeted in colonial medical, missionary, and administrative discourses. The main cause of their cultural, moral, and cognitive fixation was Christian missionary orientalism, which had the overarching goal of proselityzing the East in order to redeem it. They depicted Muslim women in the 19th century as a group that were seen as homogenous and unchanging. They were chiefly reviled for their "ignorance" and gendered "sufferings" in the lack of a good saviour like Jesus. 'Thus, in a broader sense, Muslim women in South Asia looked permanently docile and passive carriers of imposed social and cultural dictates, remaining mute spectators for their lack of ability to claim an autochthonous selfhood.' The orientalist writers viewed Muslim women as a forlorn group who had been 'immured forever in a living grave' and blamed Muhammad for

---

19. Cohn, Bernard S. 1996. *Colonialism and its Forms of Knowledge.* Princeton: Princeton University Press.

sweeping 'away forever all hope of happiness for Muslim women.'[20] Contrary to her own depiction, many Muslim women could be seen smoking cigarettes and working at diverse vocations, including producing cigarettes and knitting socks across Islamic lands.

Early orientalists of the 17th century, on the other hand, did not perceive the "hijab" (head scarf) Muslim women wore as a symbol of oppression, but rather as a piece of everyday attire with which they were content to live This is due to the fact that head scarves were a staple of women's clothing in other religions, particularly Christianity and Judaism, during the medieval and early modern periods. While Islam imposed tougher sartorial constraints for common women outside their own homes, Christian and Jewish women also had the obligation to cover their heads and hair, in order to appear modest[21] In one of her notable studies on Muslim women as imagined in western literary discourses, Mohja Kahf demonstrates that "she" was not portrayed in literature of the Middle Ages wearing a veil and living alone. These authors were too busy rescuing her 'as a Christian or a European' to pay attention to 'her inherent alienness.' It was meaningless to associate the veil only with Muslim women because Catholics and Jews continued to wear similar attire. This trend persisted up until the 17th century, when the veil and the harem were introduced as the two permanent features in Muslim women's daily

20. Griffith, M E Hume.1909. *Behind the Veil in Persia and Turkish Arabia: An account of An English Woman's Eight Years Residence Amongst the Women of the East*. London: JB Lippincott Company, 218; 222-223.

21. Goitein, SD. 1979. 'The Sexual Mores of the Common People.' In *Society and the Sexes in Medieval Islam*, edited by Afaf Lutfi Al-Sayyid-Marsot, 43-62. California: Undena Publications.

existence. According to Kahf, the rise of the trope of the 'oppressed Muslim woman' coincided with the expansion of the British and French empires in the nineteenth century. Because they had subjugated entire Muslim societies, these empires had a direct stake in portraying the Muslim woman as oppressed—even as their policies oppressed real, live Muslim women across the empires.[22]

Imperial writers suppressed the complex histories of the headscarves and ignored the reality that Muslim women's fashion choices were never uniform. Aside from the necessity to be concerned with "modesty," a phrase that is interpreted differently depending on the period and circumstance, there was little homogeneity in Muslim women's attire across the world. In the early centuries of Islam, many women wore headscarves. As Islam became a worldwide religion, women began to be portrayed, and lived, in distinct ways under various Islamic regimes. Patriarchal, priestly, and kingly control grew stronger during the Umayyad era, and contrary to what the prophet Muhammad had envisioned as the norm, women's bodies and mobility had drastically changed throughout the Islamic/Islamicate regions. Even so, women continued to live with multiple vestimentary choices that included ezar (long coats), jilbab (head cover), hebrah (Yemeni coats), khemar (Quranic scarf), shawl (face and neck cover), maganna (headscarf included chin), thattam (Kerala head cover), duppatta (open cloth for face and bosom), and saraqush (cap and scarf). Scholars have pointed out the inherent class and social hierarchy, and material circumstances associated with Islamic veiling and headscarves, and there is broad agreement that ordinary

---

22. Kahf, Mohja. 1999. *Western Representations of the Muslim Woman: From Termagant to Odalisque*. Austin: University of Texas Press, 5-6.

Muslim women in most Islamic and Islamic regions have gone unveiled from the early days of Islam, when in any case, strict veiling (full body covering) was never imposed.

Sartorial conflicts and vestimentary regulations (specifically, "covering" and "uncovering") became a significant part of the theological discourse throughout the Indian Ocean and Mediterranean Islam in the late 19th century as the new reformist forces swept throughout the Muslim world. This is the context in which Ashraf Tanawi pushed for strict veiling in all situations, including marriages, in his renowned work *Bihishti Zewar*, one of the most prominent pietistic manuals of the 19th century.[23] This text gives a range of pictures about working Muslim women, rich women with expensive clothes and jewelry, and their attempt to create their own social and gender spaces. He talks about the north Indian Muslim habitus and the "relatively privileged" households in the early 20th century, where women were mostly found unveiled in the households, and were not very strict about veiling on festive occasions like marriages.[24]

Tanawi was not the only one who purportedly feared tainted piety, which many believed to be a result of the Indians' intimate relationships with the colonizers. His pietistic manual came out immediately after Shib Chunder Bose's famous book *The Hindoos As They Are*, which was both instructive and prescriptive at the same time. Face veiling, according to Bose, was a significant indicator of female piety and marital purity in Bengali Hindu households.

---

23. Metcalf, Barbara D. 1990. *Perfecting Muslim Women, Maulana Ashraf Ali Thanawi's Bihishti Zewar*. Berkely: University of California Press, 123.

24. Ibid., 122-123.

Young brides were under strict orders to sit modestly, veil fully, and speak sparingly, if at all, to young girls of their own age.[25] He is quite clear about the need for female modesty and the importance of covering one's entire body when in public, as he considered this to be a time when Bengali Baboos were becoming more and more "corrupted" as the colonizing British took over their culture. In his attempt to at least save these Baboos' female kith and kin, Bose wrote, 'Instead of Dacca Taercha or Bale Boota sari, they must have either Benares gold embroidered or French embossed gossamer sari, with gold-lace borders and ends. It would be a very desirable improvement in the way of decency to introduce among the Hindoo women of Bengal a stouter fabric in place of the present thin, flimsy, loose muslin sari, without any other covering over it.' Bose seemed to have lost hope in the irredeemably corrupt wealthy Hindu men whose mansions 'frequently had a western-style dressing room, complete with a wardrobe made in England, adjacent to the master's bedroom in the outer apartment of the house. There the master would change into Hindu clothes before entering the inner apartment and courtyard, the province of the women and the deities of the house.'[26] Such vestimentary emulation continued to increase, despite the fact that and the colonizers felt great discomfort in seeing Indians wearing European dress and speaking English in their presence.[27] Equally, this is also a time when alongside other disciplinary practices, imperial

25. Bose, Shib Chunder. 1883. *The Hindoos as they Are: A Description of the Manners, Customs, and Inner Life of Hindoo Society in Bengal.* Calcutta: Thacker, Spik and Co, 80.

26. Cohn, 131.

27. Chaudhuri, N.C. 1976. *Culture in a Vanity Bag.* Bombay: Jaico Publishing House.

violence reached the colonised body through imposing a special dressing code for their workers.

Unveiling and Re-veiling

One of the most significant and dramatic turning points in Egypt's progressive rejection of the veil occurred in 1923 when Huda Sharawi, a well-known Egyptian feminist, ceremoniously threw her veil into the Mediterranean on her way back from a women's convention in Rome.[28] Within a decade, Egypt's veil was all but gone. According to Stillman the uncovering in Egypt received significant government support when the Fatwa Committee of al-Azhar, the foremost institution of Sunni Islamic higher learning, decided in 1937 that the Hanafi legal school, which represented the majority rite in Egypt and the Levant, was not against uncovering. It was further noted that the Maliki school, which was the foremost rite in the Maghreb and had a considerable representation in Egypt, did not see veils as an essential vestimentary auxiliary.[29] Thus, based on her experience growing up in a country with a mainly Muslim population, such as Egypt, Leila Ahmed contends that before the Islamic resurgence in the 1970s, piety and the hijab did not have a particularly close link in most areas. Many deeply devout women in these civilizations were comfortable walking uncovered and rarely donned the hijab.[30] Interestingly, Ahmed finds hope in the new-sartorial Muslim women who are highly skilled at their jobs and at the forefront of working for issues that concern religious

28. Stillman, Yedida Kalfon. 2003. *Arab Dress: From the Dawn of Islam to Modern Times*. Leiden: Brill.

29. Ibid., 155-156.

30. Ahmed, Leila. 2011. *A Quiet Revolution, The Veil's Resurgence, from the Middle East to America*. London: Yale University Press, 8.

and cultural minorities, migrants, and other oppressed people, continuing the tradition of civil rights movements and feminism in their own cultural contexts. Ahmed begins with a deep apprehension about the resurgence of hijab and veils in the Middle East and the western world.

From the early 20th century, the hijab's meaning, shape, and trend continued to evolve. Anthropologists from the colonial era perceived it as a dehumanising object. In the 1940s, the hijab was seen as an anti-Western, and pious object, in nations like Egypt. Following the decline of the Muslim Brotherhood in the 1960s, they vanished once more. In Iran, women began to wear the hijab once more in the 1970s, but in most of South Asia, it was only a symbolic covering for Muslim women who ventured outside. It was since the early 90s that headscarves became a visible sartorial trend in many Islamic societies in South Asia, and countries like India witnessed a growing trend along with the global war on "terrorism" which uncovered the dormant Islamophobia in many places. Leila Ahmed identifies several factors that led to neo-hijabi women claiming their sartorial identity in many countries in the West, Africa, and Asia. The motivations included anti-sexism, minority justice, battling prejudices, and fair treatment, in addition to gender justice. Thus, the meaning of the hijab is neither uniform, nor does it have a single history of religious affiliation, and Muslim women's justifications for wearing it have been evolving over time. Contrary to common assumptions, veiled women in the West, the Middle East, and South Asia have become outspoken advocates for marital equality and have taken the lead on matters pertaining to women's rights.[31]

---

31. Read, Jen'nan Ghazal, and John P. Bartkowski. 2000. 'To Veil or Not to Veil? A Case Study of Identity Negotiation among Muslim Women Living in Austin, Texas.' *Gender & Society*, 14 (3): 395-417.

Thus, according to Elizabeth Fernea, the hijab 'means different things to different people within [Muslim] society, and it means different things to Westerners than it does to Middle Easterners.'[32] Many European Muslim women wear the hijab as they feel that their cultural identity is under attack by the majoritarian cultural symbols; as Ellen Wiles shows, they resort to the hijab to assert the relevance of minority cultural symbols as well.[33] Similar to this, Muslim women in Canada dress sartorially to challenge popular perceptions of Islam as a subordinate and barbaric faith, to declare the identity and actuality of a self-assured Muslim community, and to ask for more social and political recognition.[34] The way Homa Hoodfar uses her own exquisite scarves illustrates how the significance of a scarf may vary depending on the wearer and the environment. 'My colourful scarf, however loosely, and decoratively worn, appears to my students as the veil, while the more complete veil of a practicing but culturally and biologically white Muslim who had worn the veil every day to work is seen as fashion.'[35] It is because the hijab has come to be associated with inferiority, humiliation, and backwardness all over the world—whether in American universities or the Indian educational system—discussion with neo-hijabi

---

32. Fernea, Elizabeth W. 1993. 'The Veiled Revolution.' *Everyday life in the Muslim Middle East*, edited by D. L. Bowen and E. A. Early. Bloomington: Indiana University Press, 122.

33. Wiles, Ellen. 2007. 'Headscarves, Human Rights, and Harmonious Multicultural Society: Implications of the French Ban for Interpretations of Equality.' *Law and Society Review*, 41(3): 699-735.

34. Hoodfar, Homa. 1993. 'The Veil in Their Minds and on Our Heads: The Persistence of Colonial Images of Muslim women.' *Resources for Feminist Research*, 22 (3/4): 5-18.

35. Ibid., 15.

women reveals that the very reason many of them wear it is because they want to shatter this stereotype.[36] Several chapters in this volume address this issue. This creates two situations: first, we see neo-hijabi women who are self-assured that they can outsmart or catch up with anyone in their chosen field; second, we see a Muslim woman who is extremely politically aware and sensitive as well as knowledgeable about her rights under the constitution and modern secular democracy.

One of the main criticisms of the headscarf has been centred on its "otherness"—the clothing itself is of Arab-Islamic origin and is incompatible with the ideal public appearances in non-Muslim regions like the West and India. As it is currently widely understood, this argument has little bearing on history. Clothes, clothing, and fashion tastes have the capacity to transcend, just like food and culinary practices, and they never stay static. The spread of the hijab was greatly inspired by the vestmental traditions that were extensively practised throughout the Arabian Peninsula as well as in Iran and Africa. Before Islam, Hellenic Greece had a significant influence on the Arab vestimentary system, and the fashion trends in Yemen and Africa in the middle ages had a significant impact on Indian Ocean communities. From the 16th century, upper-class women and men in India, from Rajasthan to the Deccan, emulated Mughal dress designs, which in turn had been influenced by the Mongols and the Chinese. In other words, the entire feudal/martial nobility of Hindustan, practiced different forms of

---

36. Haddad, Yvonne Yazbeck. 1991. 'American Foreign Policy in the Middle East and its Impact on the Identity of Arab Muslims in the United States.' *The Muslims of America*, edited by Y.Y. Haddad. Oxford, UK: Oxford University Press.

sartorial mimicry. Additionally, we observe the introduction of clothing styles from the frontier courts into the Mughal courts, particularly during Akbar's reign. Similarly, early records indicate that yellow silk clothing brought from India was highly prized as a vestibule of luxury at the Islamic Umayyid court in the early years of Islam, and that futa, a long garment imported from India, was highly prized in Islamic Arabia prior to the religion's encounter with India.[37]

Why this Anthology

This is perhaps the first time that a volume of this kind has been compiled. While the immediate provocation was the hijab ban in Karnataka, and the need to respond to it, the more important part of this exercise is to forefront the need for a historical, ethnographic and political understanding while engaging problems of contemporary significance. The essays in this volume indicate the ways in which many issues, both contemporary and historical, come together to create the grounds for the recent ban. As the contributors demonstrate, this apparently local ban needs to be read both within the wider context of minoritization of Muslims in India, as it does in post 9/11 international contexts. The apparently universally accepted dictum that the hijab is an instrument of Islamic patriarchy, intended to oppress Muslim women, is of very recent vintage and can be traced back to the US state departments that knitted together political exigency with racialized prejudice to naturalize this idea. Once produced it could be utilized within narratives about freeing Muslim women, removing Islamic backwardness, fight "terror," restore secularism or democratize countries

---

37. Stillman, 2003, 49.

with a majority Muslim population. Most such discourses chose to mobilise ideas apparently derived from secularism or feminism.

The essays here have been loosely clubbed into sections. The first, 'Context and Questions,' locates the hijab ban in three contexts—an increasingly saffronizing Karnataka, the status of uniforms and clothing in schools and their relationship to the larger cultural project of the state, and the contentious status of the task of "integrating" Muslims into the larger framework of the country, and the long standing discomfort with the presence of Muslims in public life, which is now more complicated with the growth of hardening communal lines in the country, and global Islamophobia (Nair; Sharma and Bhaskaran; Ahmed). These essays address the inadequacy of simplistic understandings of Indian secularism, and point to the need to engage the short- and long-term reasons for the growth, and normalization, of hyper masculine Hindutva politics in India.

The second section 'Reading the Ban,' opens up different ways to read the hijab ban—of whether sartorial diversity linked to religious or community differences can cause any harm; the ways in which politicizing the hijab has had a detrimental effect on Muslim women's sovereignty over their bodies, affecting their ability to live fulfilling lives; the immense diversity of reasons, from assertion, autonomy, social mobility, political consciousness, constitutional literacy, to the elements of piety that contribute to a younger generation of Indian Muslim woman wearing the hijab; and the ways in which the insistence on the importance of the uniform in the recent hijab ban can be transposed to a bigger agenda of the BJP—that of bringing in the Uniform Civil Code (Fazal; Saedi; Arafath; Arunima).

Contributors in the third section, 'Ethno/History/Life Writing,' look at the reasons for Muslim women choosing to wear or abandon the hijab; the importance of anti-communal education in schools and the ways in which this moulds attitudes; the ways in which Muslim women see their educational aspirations being threatened by the ban; on why Muslim identified clothing styles are singled out and banned; and the ways in which Muslim girls and young women have managed their own aspirations and familial desires by sometimes conforming to, and at other times resisting expected sartorial practices, without facing particularly dire consequences from the family or community (Shilujas; Dutta; Singh; Devika; Alqadar).

The anecdotal and ethnographic details speak predictably to the diversity of ways in which Muslim girls and women live and speak, and this is developed in the last section, 'Many Feminisms.' Contributors to this section express a diversity of opinions including that all religions are oppressive and the need to address bigger issues regarding Muslim education and employment, and not simply of whether a hijab is to be worn or removed; the need to listen to Muslim women's voices while discussing issues central to their lives, which is often ignored by liberal feminism; the dangers that an educated, and aware, hijab-clad Muslim woman poses to Hindutva especially as she chooses to wear the hijab to resist minoritizing; the dangerous ways in which Hindutva ideologues have utilized discourses of secularism and feminism to demonize Muslim women in hijabs and further the cause of right wing majoritarianism; and the urgent need for feminist activists to protect the rights of women without becoming complicit in larger right wing political projects (Zaheer; Jamil; Aziz; Salim; Siddiqui). The volume ends with a story by Noor Zaheer.

Read together, the essays in this volume produce a compelling argument for a historically and politically nuanced critique of the complex global phenomenon of Islamophobia. We would suggest that this is the only way to safeguard rights of minorities, embrace difference, and ensure real forms of justice and citizenship.

PART ONE

CONTEXT AND QUESTIONS

THE HIJAB AND THE INVISIBLE MUSLIM

Janaki Nair

How did the issue of six hijab wearing young women in one college in Udipi become swiftly nationalized and internationalized as the sign of a "progressive" Hindu push against the tyrannies of Muslim patriarchy? How, moreover, were fervent cries successfully made for a "secularised" classroom exactly at the time when every aspect of public and social life in the state of Karnataka has been communalized? The ceaseless attacks by Hindu groups such as the Bajrang Dal and Sri Rama Sene, the VHP, the Hindu Janajagruti Samiti, and the myriad "outfits" spawned by the Rashtriya Swayam Sevak Sangh on Muslim beliefs, practices, and now livelihoods, reveals the larger frame within which the hijab issue became the tipping point.

It would be too facile to tie the frenzied hyperactivity of these groups over the last two months to mere electoral plans. The actions reveal that the state's leaders are carrying out, with the zeal of new converts, the mandate of their masters in Delhi/Nagpur. That the attack on Karnataka's minorities is sustained, relentless, and widely endorsed by nearly all public institutions in the state today speaks of very clear long term goals that cannot risk the uncertainties of electoral politics. But the question still remains of how and why Karnataka has taken the lead in realizing Hindu Rashtra. And what place does the campaign against hijab have in this narrative?

Let us take the BJP government under the relatively new leadership of Basavaraj Bommai as Chief Minister. What began with the passage of swingeing laws—relating to cow slaughter in 2020, the regularization of unauthorized (read Hindu) religious structures on public property, or proposed changes to "conversion" laws in 2021—has turned under his leadership into daily, state-sanctioned assaults on the faith, beliefs, lives and livelihoods of Muslims. Since seizing power in 2019, the BJP in Karnataka has strained every nerve to proceed at a fast and furious pace towards the larger RSS goal of creating Hindu Rashtra. As in the passing of the Karnataka Prevention of Slaughter and Preservation of Cattle Act, 2020, with the conspicuous and unprecedented conduct of a "cow puja" in the legislature building. Or in ramming through the Legislative Assembly the ironically termed Protection of the Right to Freedom of Religion bill 2021 which goes much further than other similar acts in interfering in interfaith marriages and targeting institutions whose licences can be suspended on mere suspicion of "conversion." Chief Minister Basavaraj Bommai's response to each and every communal provocation (against Christians in Mangalore, for instance) is to restate his obedience to the men who rule the streets. He has taken the unprecedented step of granting official State compensation of ₹25 lakhs to the family of Harsha, a rowdy sheeter, whose murder even the Minister in charge of Shimoga had said was a result of enmities with his former jail mates. Such state compensation is probably a first by any Indian Chief Minister. Harsha's murder was, meanwhile, linked to his "campaign" against hijab, among other worthy actions in which he engaged.

The legislative overdrive continued in the quick and unanimous passage of the Karnataka Religious Structures (Protection) Act in September 2021. It was prompted by the belated fulfillment of a 2009 Supreme Court order to demolish 93 illegal religious structures identified at public places, including roads, junctions and parks, in Mysore district. The new act was 'considered necessary to provide for protection of religious constructions on a public place constructed before the date of commencement of this Act, in order to protect communal harmony and not to hurt the religious sentiments of the public...' while allowing the District Administration to allow 'religious activity in such protected structures subject to custom, law, usage and any other conditions as may be laid down by the State Government from time to time.' Mysuru-Kodagu MP Pratap Simha helpfully clarified matters when he said, 'Churches and Mosques cannot be weighed equally with Temples as they are just prayer halls.'

Under the leadership of the Home Minister Araga Jnanendra, who does not miss a chance to villianise Muslims, the police have proved ready and willing partners in fostering the neo-nation. When staff at two police stations, Kaup in Dakshin Kannada and Vijayapura in Bijapur, flaunted saffron clothing on Vijayadashami day in 2021, they went unpunished, in ironic contrast to the insistence on uniforms in classrooms. Reports are now emerging of police refusal to file a case against Chandru Moger of the Hindu Janajrguthi Samiti, who called for an economic boycott of Muslim fruit traders, citing possible disturbance to communal harmony, just as they move with alacrity against those protesting alarming and unchecked communal actions. They have thus shed the fig leaf of neutrality and declared their allegiance to the cause of Hindu Rashtra.

The media revealed its commitment to the Hindu cause when it assaulted Muslim students and teachers wearing hijab to educational institutions on camera, following the interim order of the High Court in February 2022. The barrage of toxic and suggestive programming on TV, as well as on social media, has been tinged with a certain righteousness.

In all this, the judiciary has remained ambiguous, either publicly espousing the Hindutva cause, (as in the decision of the Raichur Court to celebrate Republic Day using Bharata Mata rather than portraits of Gandhi or Ambedkar), averting its eyes from violations of the law by legislators, while offering them protection from "disruptive" protest.

How did Karnataka succumb so quickly to this muscular display of corrosive masculinity? The RSS worked hard over the last 100 years to achieve its goal of polarizing people on the west coast, where the economically successful Muslim has a presence. But what of the rest of Karnataka, where a mixture of induced fear and whole-hearted participation by the majority seems to be achieving the same effect? How has Hindu Rashtra become the sole visionary future for legions of young people? For one, there is a new and passionate righteousness to the language and gestures of the men, and some women, who participated in the harassment of Christian prayer groups last year, or willingly wore orange shawls in February this year. The giddy sense of psychic empowerment arises alongside gnawing awareness that education alone is no longer the guarantee of social mobility. Second, there is utter disarray among those social groups, and within those social movements—the Dalit Sangarsh Samiti, the farmers' and the women's movement—that had made Karnataka the site of novel social justice and development measures in the recent past. The brief flicker of a pushback, by Dalit men wearing blue shawls in Chitradurga at the height of the hijab protests, was swiftly suppressed. Thirdly, the cultural capital which could have been the basis for a vigorous regional pushback—the Kannada language—appears exhausted, given the aggressive demand for English, the growing presence of Hindi, and increasing state support for Sanskrit. Karnataka's network of socially progressive Lingayat mathas, which have functioned like alternative governments in their respective regions, have preferred to retain their autonomy with their tacit support of Hindutva.

Following the prohibition by college managements in coastal Karnataka (and now elsewhere as well) of the use of the hijab in classrooms by young women students, BJP leaders and ministers in particular took great pride in being the purveyors of "secularism" in the classroom. Girls (and now boys have been conveniently added) should come to the college to study and not to assert their cultural/ethnic/religious identities or differences. At first glance, this seems like a blameless injunction—only the unmarked "secular" citizen/subject and the "uniformity" of the classroom can engage in the true pursuit of knowledge, and buttress a constitutional democracy such as ours. Now, armed with a High Court Order which has made uniforms the norm in colleges, the state makes itself out to be the robust protectors of law and order.

Yet, as we have seen, public space and public discourse

in Karnataka is suffused with neo-Hinduness. The invocation
by Home Minister, Araga Jnanendra, and the court, of the
"secular" space of the classroom is, therefore, not just
ironic, but diabolical in intent. It "rescues" the Muslim
woman, oppressed by a patriarchal Islam of which the hijab
is the prime marker, from her captors. Having for so long
and loudly proclaimed, along with CT Ravi, Pratap Simha,
K Eswarappa, Tejaswi Surya and myriad other elected BJP
MPs and MLAs, that Hindu culture was in danger, the
honourable Home Minister, while fearlessly sporting a red
mark on his forehead, offers the Muslim woman "secular"
protection in the classroom. It is into this same classroom
that instruction in the Bhagavad Gita will be introduced.

As two spirited protests in Bengaluru, one on March 8
itself, asserted, the hijab issue was about Muslim women's
right to education. Their hard-won place in the classroom
cannot be snatched away by either the Hindu or Muslim
patriarchs. Whether Muslim women choose to wear the
hijab or not—and let us be clear that both of these can
be subversive actions at this time—they deserve their space
as citizens of this democratic republic. They must fear
neither their new "protectors" nor their adversaries. But
for now, faced with the phalanx of institutions—of the
Government, the law, the police, the media, and college
managements themselves—that are ranged against them,
when the "second-classness" of Karnataka Muslims has
been declared in all but law, their struggles will be long
and protracted. Women's is the longest revolution indeed.

LEARNING SAMENESS, RECOGNIZING DIFFERENCES

Lessons from Karanataka

Navneet Sharma and Harikrishnan Bhaskaran

Humans learn conceptual relationships such as sameness and difference as higher cognitive schemas. Oranges and apples are different but have the sameness of being a fruit akin to men and women of different colour, races, nationality, religion, caste, and sexuality being humans. Many others with specific traits and attributes share the sameness of being human. This understanding or learning does not obstruct, but rather promotes self-actualization, an ultimate aim of any and every educative process. School or any learning institution must be a place to confront the humanity of others. Uniforms in schools have a long history and were introduced to teach equality via sameness. It is not to argue that children consciously experience uniforms as "uniforming" but that uniforms and their foregoing policies assume that confronting strangers or 'others' will instil deeper differences in younger minds, thus seeing sameness is given more importance instead of recognizing the difference. Recognizing difference may also lead to a cry for redistribution or may promote the politics of difference. Uniforms attempt not only to craft an imaginary uniformity or sameness but also are what Nancy Fraser calls a bivalent concept of social justice that bridges the divide between the spheres of distribution and recognition.

Policymakers and authorities tell us that uniforms can help minimize disruptive behaviour, remove socio-economic tension and also contribute to achieving high academic standards. The uniforms are hardly expected to and do not address socio-economic differences or cure disruptive behaviour, but they only "dress" them. The ideal of impartiality is given to reckon with the idea of uniforms. Impartiality of assessment and response by teachers, the neutrality of behaviour amongst students, academic achievement, juvenile delinquency, gender appropriateness, race relations, gang affiliations were some of the concerns when "uniforms" were thought of and when the school became accessible to everyone as an institution of mass education. Soon, schools and other learning institutions became the site for the practice of "disciplinary power." Foucault, in his analysis of power, besides prison had school as the site where "discipline" is administered. Pupils' time, movement, and behaviours are tightly controlled through timetables and dress. The uniform in this context emerges as a tool prescribing and micromanaging children's behaviour and thus making them "objects of control."

The detailed regulations and vocabulary with which uniforms are specified and prescribed are evidence of how uniforms play a role in the disciplinary mechanism. Besides homogenizing and hierarchizing boys and girls, one can see the attempt to "discipline" girls more than boys. How the shirt needs to be buttoned up and the length of skirts needs to reach below knee, the kind of plaits, pony to be tied with specific ribbons, no high-heels, jewellery, accessories, make-up, etc. and also the prescribed haircut for boys and to be clean-shaven, these prescriptions not only exclude everything that does not conform to rigid schemas including non-traditional gender expressions but also is an attempt to make "good" and docile students/citizens. Simultaneously, age group, leadership (prefect, house captains), and other probable distinctions can be marked with different prescribed uniforms. Many schools and now even colleges and university departments (especially MBA ones) justify the wearing of uniforms as it adds to pupils' "human capital" and is in their interest as future competitors in the job market. The appearance and uniforms make one look professional and increase the chance of employability. School uniforms are also reminiscent of the typical work dress of white-collar jobs and thus also instill the idea of which kind of jobs are worth striving for.

The recent pandemic-induced closures of school campuses could not even take away the disciplinary mechanism of uniforms. Even to attend online classes from the confines of home, students were expected to don the uniforms to feel more "disciplined" and "connected" with their respective schools. Affordability and the need of donning uniforms at home did not become an issue with the "rich" discourse that evolved quickly about online learning, hybrid learning, and the inevitability of learning with the help of technology alone.

Besides the row over what kind of uniforms are to be worn on a regular basis, there is a raging controversy about the attire to be worn on convocation. Caps and gowns or robes were considered too colonial and UGC "suggested" replacing it with "dress" more appropriate with our "climatic and cultural" conditions. The attempt to decolonize education considered replacing uniforms more important than altering the epistemic discourse and pedagogy. Moreover, given the vastness and multiplicities of geography and culture, the attempt was seen as an enforcement of the "saffron" idea of discipline and governmentality.

Karanataka's Udupi Hijab row may have started as a crude attempt by a few to grab limelight, but it snow-balled into a state-level issue soon. An assembly election early next year will perhaps keep it simmering. However, this has re-centered the debate on "appropriate" uniform and its disciplinary mechanism. It is not a confrontation between school dress and religious dress per se. Otherwise, the tilak or turban worn by Hindus and Sikhs would also have been objected to. It is a majoritarian stance which attempts to keep politics of intolerance and the 80:20 debate alive.[1]

In India, this is perhaps the first instance when a state government took such an aggressive stance toward the symbolic clothing of a particular religious community resulting in communal tension across the region. There are several instances in the past where educational institutions or the State were challenged by individuals for prescribing specific dress codes or practices which affected their religious

---

1. During the campaign for the assembly elections in the UP in 2022, the incumbent chief Minister Yogi Adityanath spoke at a Doordarshan conclave. 'It will be an 80% versus 20% in UP polls and the BJP will retain power,' he said. Later he denied that the comment was not in the context of any religion. Apparently, Muslims constitute roughly 20% of the population in UP. (For details, see HT Correspondent, "Yogi's '80%-20%' remark bid to inflame communal tension: Oppn." *Hindustan Times*, January 11, 2022 https://www.hindustantimes.com/india-news/yogis-80-20-remark-bid-to-inflame-communal-tension-oppn-101641839851465. html

beliefs or practices. The case of the school students who declined to chant the national anthem citing their religious beliefs or the case of the Muslim students challenging the CBSE's decision not to allow hijabs or full-sleeve clothing for appearing in the All India Premedical Entrance in 2016 are some of such instances. None of these cases triggered widespread communal tensions or a vindictive approach from the State. The issue of symbolic clothing related to religious identity and cultural practice and its accommodation in the general public sphere and educational institutions is not a debate exclusive to India. There have been instances and debates about restricting symbolic clothing in public places in France, Turkey and other parts of the European Union. Similarly, educational institutions in different states in the US have differing norms on what kind of symbolic clothing (religious or otherwise) is allowed in educational spaces.

Gereluk (2004) examined the spectrum of arguments usually applied for restricting symbolic clothing in educational institutions. She identifies four major arguments used in the ban of symbolic clothing in common schools. One of these is to 'preserve the public sphere,' be it the collective national identity or its secular nature. Exponents of this principle posit that symbolic clothing leads to losing the specific collective, national identity or the secular or civic republican nature of the society. The other three arguments used for banning symbolic clothing can be termed as the offensive principle, oppressive principle and disruptive principle. According to the proponents of the oppressive principle, symbolic clothing can be banned if it is offensive. Similarly, in some instances, symbolic clothing in educational institutions is seen as either oppressing people who wear it or others. This is often cited as a reason for banning symbolic clothing. The disruptive principle posits that some kinds of symbolic clothing may have disruptive potential as far as the normal functioning of the society or the institution is concerned. Gereluk (2004) argues that these logics are arbitrary for several reasons. First of all, clearly defining what constitutes a shared national identity is not possible in a culturally diverse context. Similarly, defining what kind of symbolic clothing can possibly threaten the secular or national identity is a challenging task since the national and secular identity of a nation cannot be a single monolithic expression. The case is same when it comes to defining what constitutes offensive, oppressive or disruptive symbolic clothing.

In the Karnataka hijab row, the State and the extra-state elements have anchored the hijab ban exactly on these four arguments. This is reflected in the orders issued by the state government, the stand of the advocate general who represented the State in the case and the high court's interpretation of the merit of the arguments of the plaintiffs. These arguments were also manifested in the social media narratives shaped around the incident.

In the present instance, the "ban" manifests in the form of multiple documents from the State. The order issued by the state government on 5th February 2022 states that the institutions have the right to decide their uniform policies and in cases where such policies are not issued, students should wear something which 'would accord with equality & integrity and would not disrupt the public order.' An interim decision by the high court ruled that 'pending consideration of all these petitions, we restrain all the students regardless of their religion or faith from wearing saffron shawls (Bhagwa), scarfs, hijab, religious flags or the like within the classroom, until further orders.' The third instance is the final verdict by the high court on 15th March 2022 in which it concluded that wearing the hijab is not an essential part of the religious practice. It also found no fault with the above-mentioned government order or in educational institutions or College Development Committees (CDCs) deciding the dress codes for the students in respective institutions. The petitioners have appealed against this verdict in the Supreme Court which is still pending as of this writing.

How the state discursively shaped and validated the four arguments against symbolic clothing on school premises while ignoring the principle of reasonable accommodation is worth examining to further the discussion on how the Karnataka hijab row manifests as an instance of strategic use of popular logic to further an ideological project.

For instance, the order issued by the state government agency delegating College Development Committees the power to decide the dress code of respective Pre-University colleges is cited as an instance of exercising the provisions under the 1983 Act which calls for 'cultivating scientific and secular outlook through education.' The order also alludes that in case such policies have not been formulated, students should wear attire that ensures equality and integrity and that the attire should not cause social disruption. Read in the context of the hijab ban, the order and the state submission in the court discursively use the principles of preserving the social identity when it alludes to the hijab being against the secular outlook, equality and integrity of the student folk. The move, according to the submission, is a way to promote the spirit of 'harmony and common brotherhood' beyond 'religious, linguistic, regional and sectional diversities.' Furthermore, it uses the disruptive argument by prescribing that the attire should not disrupt public order.

The state response also uses the oppressive argument to further its hijab ban. The submission says that the move is necessary to instill freedom and dignity and to discourage practices that are derogatory to the dignity of women. The practice, according to the State, amounts to disrobing the individual choice of Muslim women if it is not an essential practice of religion. It further compares the practice of hijab to the practice of triple talaq to allude that Indian courts have shifted their practice when it comes to dealing with what is an essential religious practice.

These principles are further examined by the court as part of its final judgment where it concludes that considering the hijab or bhagwa as religiously sacrosanct and unquestionable, could work against instilling scientific temperament in students. At one point, the court observes that students, if given the autonomy to pick their attire, would 'only breed indiscipline' and chaos on the campus and in the society.

These arguments are often used against cultural and religious minorities that are at the margins in such a way as to disadvantage them further. Addressing this issue, Gereluk (2004) tries to define reasonable accommodation as a way to ascertain what schools can do to avoid inequitable treatment of the marginalized minorities. According to her, four considerations can be used for understanding the reasonable accommodation of symbolic clothing: Institutions should consider if the symbolic clothing in question causes any health and safety issues or if it is oppressive or inhibits the educational aims. Finally, it should be considered if the clothing is an essential part of the student's identity.

Considering the hijab ban from these tenets of reasonable accommodation, it can be seen that the health and safety factor does not arise in the case of the hijab issue at all. As it is also applicable to other kinds of clothes, alterations, instead of a ban, would be a more viable option. She also argues that offensive and oppressive clothing like T-shirts carrying racial slurs should be banned since it is oppressive and offensive to others. However, the oppressive nature should be supported by evidence. For instance, she observes that an anti-hijab stand by the French government caused more Muslim girl students to start wearing hijab as part of expressing their identity, protest and solidarity. In this case, contrary to the popular belief, the argument of the hijab being oppressive to Muslim girl students was not supported by evidence.

If symbolic clothing restricts the teaching-learning process, it may be considered a criterion to contemplate a change. Gereluk (2004) points out certain symbolic clothing like the niqab as a case of symbolic clothing impacting educational aims. Since the niqab does not allow seeing the face and mouth of the student, it may negatively impact language learning. However, such an issue does not arise in the case of the hijab.

Patriarchal norms such as veiling and gender-based discrimination may well exist as part of religious practices. However, such oppression manifest in terms of evidence (socio-economic indicators, health indicators, etc.) as well. For instance, social marginalization of under-privileged sections of the society in the form of caste-discrimination in India manifest in several ways as documented evidence, be it their presence in the decision-making positions in the governance system or the quality of life they enjoy.

Identifying such evidence to support a hijab ban would have made the situation different. However, taking a vindictive stand rather than exploring ways of reasonable accommodation through alternatives will eventually put the disadvantaged gender group at a greater disadvantage and lead to further oppression. In this case, girl students who refused to remove their hijab have lost their chances to appear in the final examinations. Many girl students who hail from religious families in the minority community may be denied schooling since going to school without a hijab is against religious beliefs and practices. This is where reasonable accommodation turns out important.

For instance, Kendriya Vidyalayas in India have a policy that facilitates reasonable accommodation of students from different religious and social identities and their symbolic clothing. Hijab is not excluded in this policy but rather accommodated. Unfortunately, the Karnataka High Court observed that it is not impressed with citing the Kendriya Vidyalaya practice as a case of reasonable accommodation. Any such accommodation, according to the court would fail the idea of a homogenized uniform system which will create "social-separateness" with two kinds of students, one wearing hijab and the other without. Based on this observation, the court finds the reasonable accommodation not viable.

The state's approach in the case of hijab row and the disregard for any reasonable accommodation perhaps points to the status of symbolic clothing in schools as an issue that has the potential to further the state's ideological project of homogenizing the imagined nation. It may find instances in other parts of the country shortly as it has all the ingredients needed for the cultural integration of Hindu supremacy disguised as an argument for social equality, secularism and scientific temper in educational institutions. In the face of it, the argument that the hijab as a religious symbol is out of place in an educational institution is viable within the spectrum of a mechanistic secular argument. From this perspective, the educational institutions, as per their secular nature, should not have space for any religious symbols or practices. However, the secular practice of the State in India has long been not so secular. This is not a new normal set by the incumbent right-wing party. Its forerunner, the centre-right party with 60 plus years of ruling history—had already set in the non-secular practices in educational spaces. This comes in the form of Saraswati poojas and Vedic hymn chants for initiating auspicious events to practices like guru pooja and havans conducted in educational spaces. While this may be a case of cultural integration, it has been used as the cultural and political capital by the Hindutva ideology to further its integration into the popular logic and practices in India. The rise of the manifest Hindutva party just intensified these integration practices and has taken this to the next level from cultural integration to cultural dominance.

For this ideological project to go forward, the assimilation of its objectives into easily acceptable popular or rather the populist logic, is vital. While the supremacy of the Virat Hindu is the actual ideological project, the modernist uber-sexual middle class in the country will be apprehensive if this primitive idea is presented in its real colours, no matter how much they find the Modi/Yogi bandwagon enchanting. Disguising it as a cultural logic that banks on a modernist idea like secularism or scientific temperament is important for the state steered by the right-wing forces

The Hijab

despite their distaste for such values. The hijab row in Karnataka perpetuates itself on this logic by anchoring on the secular argument trying to further its cultural dominance project.

School uniforms have always been problematic for the State as well as the socio-religious powers since a change in the school uniforms can also manifest in the form of a disruption of the status quo. It is evident in the recent controversy related to gender-neutral uniforms in one of the schools in Kerala. The school authorities, in consultation with the Parents Teachers Association, have decided to go for gender-neutral uniforms for the students in the school. The change, while welcomed by most of the youngsters, annoyed a section of the conservative male folk, as they found it a direct disruption of breaking existing boundaries and social norms of gender segregation. The debate went on with religious fundamentalists from all sides rooting for gender-segregated dress codes for students. It can be seen that the change here generally annoyed the conservative section, mainly the males, since the change in the dress code challenged gender representations and equations. The debate was reflected in the form of dramatic televised debates where naïve challenges were raised about males wearing a shawl or shaving their moustache and even about how women may urinate wearing trousers.

Though this issue also happened roughly at the same time as the hijab row, it did not garner much national or international attention, despite its similarity with the latter. In both cases, state or state-led institutions made a change to the dress codes of students in the educational institutions (though the former involved proper deliberations with the stakeholders involved before rolling out the decision). In both cases, there was considerable protest locally against the decision (though the nature, scale of the protest and the attention they received differed very much).

However, there was visible difference in these two incidents also. Not just in their geographical occurrence, but also in the protest that ensued. The gender-neutral uniform decision was primarily affecting the students' daily life and so they were the first stakeholders. However, most of the students who were affected by the policy change on what kind of uniform to wear were reportedly comfortable with the change. The protests which ensued were led by groups that were not directly affected by the change but were more concerned about the impact it will have on existing gender norms. The hijab row, on the contrary, was a decision that was taken without deliberation with the stakeholders involved. It was also reflected in the protest that ensued where the face of the protest were Muslim girl students who were directly impacted by the decision.

Despite these differences, only the Karnataka incident attracted national and international attention and resulted in a severe hate campaign. This is because the incident had the opportunity to set the narrative as an instance of religious fundamentalism versus secular attitude in the educational space. This logic and narrative are very convenient for the rationales of the middle-classes in India. This convenience is reflected in the response of other religious minorities and the general urban middle class to the hijab row. Many Christian groups took a stand that supports the hijab ban. This stand is derived from a perspective that sees the anti-hijab ban protests as a case of Muslim religious fundamentalism, rather than a case of protest to wear symbolic clothing which is part of religious/cultural identity.

Primarily, it is the political capital involved in the polarization potential of the narrative that makes the right-wing forces play a proactive role in setting the tone of the narrative and orchestrating hate propaganda despite their core ideological project standing against the secular logic which it strategically used in this instance. So instead of looking at it as a case of symbolic clothing and its accommodation in a diverse educational space, the narrative about the hijab row is set on the hijab as clothing that marks the Muslim identity.

However, the question of headscarves being a religious symbol (so not permissible in educational institutions) is a confusing one, especially when the question is of trying to decide whether to allow it or not. For instance, when does a headscarf turn into a hijab? Across India, especially in the Northern region, women covering their heads is a long-standing cultural practice. Though this is not an essential part of Hindu religious practice, it is followed among Hindu folk and is associated with some of their religious customs as well. Similarly, the Sikh practices require individuals to cover their heads with a scarf or turban as part of religious belief. Neck scarves are a very popular style statement among youngsters. They use it very creatively, even in places where the use of it is not warranted by the climatic conditions. In all these cases, the scarves are not hijabs. A headscarf turns into a hijab when it is worn by a Muslim woman. So the headscarf here is closely associated with the religious identity of Muslim women. Now specifically considering the hijab as a religious symbol that may disturb the peace is problematic in this instance. It points to religious identities or certain specific religious symbolic clothing gaining the potential to be provocative in the opinion of the State.

The debate is also not about the collective right (of school as an institution) versus individual rights. It is also not about liberating women from the veil, it is about the dominance of saffron angavastrams over the hijab. Arguably the rights of religious minorities to protect and preserve their language, culture, heritage, and tradition are guaranteed by the constitution which cannot be contravened by varying institutional policies concerning school uniforms. The statistics already paint a dismal picture, and accordingly a fourth of Muslim children between the ages of 6 and 14 have either never attended school or are dropouts.[2] For children above the age of 17, only 17 per cent of Muslims have done matriculation against the national average of 26 per cent. The participation of Muslims in higher education also ranges from four to five per cent. In this, the plight of Muslim women will be more dreadful than Muslim men needs no serious research. This controversy over the hijab as a uniform will obstruct the access of all *Shahbanos*[3] to schooling itself and their clamour for the required redistribution of resources and social justice.

---

2. *Social, Economic and Educational Status of the Muslim Community of India: A Report.* Prime Minister's High Level Committee Cabinet Secretariat, Government of India, 2006, p.58.

3. Shah Bano is now seen as representing a quintessential Indian Muslim woman based on the notoriety that accompanied the famous divorce-maintenance (haq-mehar) case and this case also became a quintessential case of Muslim appeasement.

References

Foucault, Michel. *The Archaeology of Knowledge*. Vintage Publication, 1982.

Gereluk, Dianne. *Symbolic Clothing in Schools: what should be worn and why*. Continuum, 2008.Sharma, N. and S.A. Mir. "Kashmir: Old Political Chimera Is Social Again." *Mainstream Weekly*, Vol.56, 2018.

HT Correspondent. "Yogi's '80%-20%' remark bid to inflame communal tension:Oppn." *Hindustan Times*, January 11, 2022, https://www.hindustantimes.com/india-news/yogis-80-20-remark-bid-to-inflame-communal-tension-oppn-101641839851465.html

Keddie, Amanda. "Schooling and social justice through the lenses of Nancy Fraser." *Critical Studies in Education*, Vol.53(3), 2012, pp.1-17. 10.1080/17508487.2012.709185.

Qamar, F. and N. Sharma. "More Muslim representation needed in higher education." *Deccan Herald*, 5 October, 2021.

Sharma, N. et.al. "Science education in India: A Misnomer for Scientific Temper." *NISCAIR-CSIR*, 2020, pp. 135-145.

Social, Economic and Educational Status of the Muslim Community of India: A Report. Prime Minister's High Level Committee Cabinet Secretariat, Government of India, 2006, p.58.

The Karnataka Education Act 1983.The Government of Karnataka. https://righttoeducation.in/sites/default/files/THE%20KARNATAKA%20EDUCATION%20ACT,%201983.pdf

POLITICS OF HIJAB

A Note

Hilal Ahmed

The hijab controversy, like many other contentious issues related to Muslim identity in India, is presented to us as a closed ended question. We are asked to choose from a set of two predefined answers: pro-hijab and/or anti-hijab. An impression is created that hijab controversy symbolizes an inevitable cultural dispute between Muslim separatism and the Indian cultural ethos. And for this reason, one has to take a definite position to confirm his/her loyalties. Interestingly, the legal response to this public debate, especially the detailed order passed by the Karnataka High Court, also has strengthened this impression. A clear dividing line between religion and public life is drawn as if hijab debate has nothing to do with Hindutva's anti-Muslim rhetoric. This imposed explanatory framework is highly misleading. It does not allow us to examine the manner in which a social phenomenon, in this case hijab, is transformed into a conflict of civilization between Islam and Hinduism.

Contextualizing the Political Questions

Let us begin with a brief overview of this debate. According to the media reports this controversy started in January 2022. Six hijab-wearing female Muslim students of a pre-University college in Udupi town of Karnataka were not allowed to attend classes on the ground that wearing Hijab was a violation of the uniform policy of the college. This refusal led to a widespread debate across the state. The Hindu rightist organizations also demanded that Hindu students should be allowed to wear saffron scarfs. In the meantime, the Karnataka government issued an Order on 5 February 2022, clarifying the official stand of the state on this matter. Reiterating the official position that no exception could be made for Muslim girls wearing hijab, the Order instructed the educational institutions to follow the strict Uniform Policy. This led to a series of protests against the government's rigid attitude. A number of petitions were also filed in the Karnataka High Court claiming that wearing hijab is an essential Islamic religious practice that is protected by the Constitution itself.

The High Court issued an Interim Order in this case on 10 February 2022. All students were asked to wear the officially prescribed uniform without any religious attire or symbol in school and pre-University colleges. This Interim Order was followed in a highly mechanical manner by the authorities. Female students, and in some cases the hijab-wearing Muslim teachers, were forced to remove their hijabs outside the gates of many schools and junior colleges. Finally, the Karnataka High Court delivered its judgement on 15 March 2022. Upholding the restrictions on hijab and other religious attires such as saffron scarfs, the Court categorically rejected the plea that wearing the hijab was an essential religious practice in Islam. In an interesting move, the Al Qaeda chief Ayman al-Zawahiri issued a video message praising the college student Muskan Khan, who defended her right to wear hijab in the classroom. Although Muskan Khan's parents denied any connection with Al-Qaeda and disassociated themselves from this video, the ruling BJP, including the Karnataka Chief minister, Basavaraj Bommai remained apprehensive of an invisible hand behind the pro-hijab protests.

There are, at least, two important issues in this story that need to be analysed rather systematically. Wearing religious symbols by young students in schools and colleges is not an unusual phenomenon. These symbols are not seen as a violation of any prescribed institutional dress-code. In many cases, these symbols are applauded in schools and educational institutions as they celebrate cultural diversity and inclusiveness. However, in this case, a very different interpretation is offered to hijab. It is defined as a problematic attire that has a potential to disturb the socio-cultural harmony in a classroom setting. In a broader sense, hijab is envisaged as a cultural threat to the defined contours of national identity that is understood here in strictly Hindu terms. One must, therefore, ask a straightforward question: what is specific to hijab that eventually transforms it into a communally-sensitive issue?

The idea of secularism is the second important aspect of this controversy. The senior BJP leaders (including the Home Minister Amit Shah, the Defence Minister Rajnath Singh and Chief Minister Basavaraj Bommai), the college authorities and even the High Court seem to agree that religious attires of any kind, especially hijab, should not be permitted in educational institutions to uphold the sanctity

of secular education.[1] Although the BJP leaders do not use
the word secularism, they evoke the old secular arguments
that religion is a matter of personal choice and it must not
have any space in public life. The question, thus, arises:
what is the nature of this secularism? And how does it
contribute to Hindutva politics?

Hijab as Muslim Politicophobia

The transformation of hijab into a political issue, in my
view, should not be reduced to what is called Islamophobia.
The term "Islamophobia" does not capture the complexities
associated with the hijab debate. Islamophobia is a western
notion that aims to address the anxieties of the white-middle
class population in the US and Europe. It refers to an
intense dislike or fear of Islam/prejudice towards Muslims.
Although one can find very similar manifestations of anti-
Islam/anti-Muslim attitude in India, there is a need to look
at the specificity of Indian debates.

We must remember that the placing of Muslim identity
in the larger schema of India's national identity has always
been a contentious issue. Despite the fact that India adopted
a secular Constitution based on the concept of unity in
diversity, the political elite has never been fully comfortable
with Muslim presence in public life. In the initial years
after the partition in 1947 it was alleged that Muslims

---

1. In an interview, Home Minister Amit Shah said: 'It is my personal
belief that people of all religions should accept the school's dress
code. And the issue is now in court, and the court is conducting its
hearings on the matter. Whatever it decides should be followed by all.'
See https://www.news18.com/news/politics/hijab-row-my-personal-belief-
that-all-religions-must-accept-school-dress-code-amit-shah-tells-news18-
in-exclusive-interview-4794080.html

did not participate in the national building process.[2] This perception was so strong that even the serious commentators of Muslim politics tend to subscribe to this view. The enthusiastic participation of Muslims in electoral politics and other sphere of public life was ignored and an image of an isolated and inward-looking Muslim community was established. A new yet equally problematic public image of Muslims began to take shape in the mid-1960s. Muslims were now envisaged as rational agents, who would always participate in electoral politics for maximizing collective, communal interests. This led to what is popularly known as the politics of the Muslim vote bank.[3] These conflicting Muslim images found completely different meanings in the post-9/11 scenario. A set of terms such as Jihadi Islam, Islamic terrorism, Sharia Rule and so on came into existence. This new and globally acceptable vocabulary of politics amalgamated with the established explanatory templates to redefine Muslim presence in global terms. The markers of Muslim identity—green minarets of mosques, use of loudspeaker for Azan, congregational namaz on roads and now hijab—which always have strong local/ regional linkages, were separated from their immediate cultural context to justify the alien character of Indian Islam. This merger between the global anti-Islamism and anti-Muslim communalism led to a new political consensus,

---

2. For a detailed discussion, see Ahmed, Hilal. 'Representing Muslims in Postcolonial India: Constitution of a Political Discourse.' *Decolonisation and the Politics of Transition in South Asia*, edited by Sekhar Bandyopadhyay, Orient Blackswan, 2016, pp. 348-374.

3. See Ahmed, Hilal. *Siyasi Muslims: A Story of Political Islams in India*. Penguin-Random House, 2019.

which may be called the Muslim politicophobia.[4]

Hijab controversy is a perfect example of Muslim politicophobia for two reasons. First, the hijab is seen as an alien influence. A clear distinction between Indian values/ religions and the foreign influence is made to reject hijab as antithesis of Indian identity. The High Court judgement is very relevant in this regard. It says:

'We notice that all was well with the dress code since 2004. We are also impressed that even Muslims participate in the festivals that are celebrated in the ashta mutt sampradaya, (Udupi being the place where eight Mutts are situated). We are dismayed as to how all of a sudden that too in the middle of the academic term the issue of hijab is generated and blown out of proportion by the powers that be.'[5]

It is important to highlight here that the judges do appreciate the participation of Muslim girl students in the ashta mutt sampradaya festivals. These ceremonies as religious acts cannot be separated from local Hindu religious traditions. Muslim participation in these Hindu ceremonies, the judgement reminds us, is not at all problematic because it reflects Muslim loyalty to Indian culture defined in Hindu religious terms. However, a different logic is invoked to assess the cultural/religious status of hijab. It is seen as an offensive religious symbol that cannot be accommodated in the local cultural milieu. The judgement also focuses on a given timeline (2004) to highlight the fact that hijab was a cultural invention by Muslim students as if their aim

---

4. In my forthcoming essay, I discuss the various aspects of Muslim politicophobia. See, Ahmed, Hilal. 'Muslim imaginations of Islam in India.' *Journal of Muslim Philanthropy and Civil Society*, Indian University, forthcoming.

5. W.P. NO.2347 OF 2022/ 15 March 2022 pp. 126-127.

was to disturb the social and religious harmony. It simply means that any expression of Muslim identity is bound to be interpreted in clear political terms.

There is an interesting story of this line of argument, especially from the point of view of Hindutva politics. Deendayal Upadhyay, the ideologue of Jan Sangh and BJP, makes an interesting observation in one of his famous lectures on Integral Humanism. He says: 'Group has its feelings too. These are not exactly similar to the individual's feelings. Group feelings cannot be considered a mere arithmetic addition of individual feelings. Group strength too is not a mere sum of individuals' strength… it is observed that Hindus even if they are rascals [in] individual life, when they come together in a group, they always think of good things. On the other hand, when two Muslims come together, they propose and approve of things which they themselves in their individual capacity would not even think of. They start thinking in an altogether different way. This is an everyday experience.'[6]

The High Court judgement, in a way, legitimizes this argument. There is a perceived fear that the collective Muslim assertion will always be counterproductive, reactionary and harmful. Hijab-wearing girls, in this sense, are seen as a Muslim challenge—a clear manifestation of Muslim politicophobia.

There is another and more profound dimension of this anxiety. The local BJP leaders and the Hindutva organizations have tried to delegitimize the anti-hijab ban. There is an argument that Muslim girls and women have started wearing hijab under the influence of Muslim

---

6. See http://avap.org.in/Uploads/Publication/Integral%20Humanism3.pdf

extremist organizations. These organizations, we are told, actually managed the protest in a systematic manner to disturb the communal harmony in the state. The High Court judgement also subscribes to this argument. It notes: 'The way, hijab imbroglio unfolded gives scope for the argument that some "unseen hands" are at work to engineer social unrest and disharmony. Much is not necessary to specify. We are not commenting on the ongoing police investigation lest it should be affected.'[7]

No one can ignore the fact that the nature of Islamic religiosity has changed in a significant way in the last two decades. This has paved the way for a new kind of Islamic visibility, which is clearly manifested in the everyday life of Muslim communities. This evolving pattern of religiosity has certainly affected the dress-code of Muslim communities, especially in South India. Similarly, there is a strong presence of Muslim organizations in South Karnataka. The Campus Front, the student wing of the Popular Front of India (PFI) was one of the first groups that led the protest against the hijab ban, even before the enactment of the controversial Government Order.[8]

These sociological and political changes, however, should not be seen as independent and self-governing phenomena. There is a much wider context that needs to be taken into consideration. We must note that the Islamic religiosity, especially in Southern states, is inextricably linked to prevalent imaginations of religion and spirituality in contemporary India. The Pew Report, Religion in India:

---

7. W.P. NO.2347 OF 2022/ 15 March 2022 pp. 126-127.

8. See https://www.telegraphindia.com/india/hijab-clad-students-denied-entry-to-classroom-in-udupi-pu-college/cid/1845798

Tolerance and Segregation is very relevant here.[9] This report shows a conflicting pattern. On the one hand, there is an extreme polarization on religious grounds that has contributed significantly to the identity formation of the members of religious groups. On the contrary, the faith in karma and astrology has increased in an unprecedent manner across the communities. This has led to a strange process of individuation.[10] It is found that the acceptance of fate and karma is an important feature of contemporary religiosity. A significant majority of respondents (70%) claim that they believe in fate—the idea that the life events of an individual are largely predetermined. Hindus (73%), Muslims (63%) and Sikhs (59%) strongly assert this view. This is also true about the belief in Karma. An influential majority comprises of Hindus (77%), Muslims (77%) and Jains (75%) strongly adhere to this Karma-oriented world-view. The interplay between these two seemingly paradoxical aspects—extreme polarization and extreme individuation—determine the nature of religiosity and community formation in different contexts. This is also true about Hindu and Muslim communities of South

---

9. The report is based on the interview of 29,999 Indian adults (including 22,975 who identify as Hindu, 3,336 who identify as Muslim, 1,782 who identify as Sikh, 1,011 who identify as Christian, 719 who identify as Buddhist, 109 who identify as Jain and 67 who identify as belonging to another religion or as religiously unaffiliated). Interviews for this nationally representative survey were conducted face-to-face from November 2019, to March 23, 2020. The questionnaire was developed in English and translated into 16 languages, independently verified by professional linguists with native proficiency in regional dialects. See https://www.pewresearch.org/religion/2021/06/29/religion-in-india-tolerance-and-segregation/

10. For a fully developed version of this argument, see Ahmed, Hilal. 'Muslim imaginations of Islam in India.' *Journal of Muslim Philanthropy and Civil Society*, Indian University, forthcoming.

Karnataka. Interestingly, the Muslim identity formation on overtly religious lines and growing Islamization are seen as a problem; while, the violent Hindu assertion of religious identity in predominately radicalized Hindutva terms is completely ignored. The recent Annual Report of the Rashtriya Swayamsevak Sangh's Akhil Bharatiya Pratinidhi Sabha is very relevant example in this regard. It says: 'The brutal murders of activists of Hindu organizations in Kerala, Karnataka are an example of this menace. Series of dastardly acts revealing communal hysteria, rallies, demonstrations, violation of social discipline, custom and conventions under the guise of the Constitution and religious freedom, inciting violence by instigating meagre causes, promoting illegal activities, etc. is increasing. There appears to be elaborate plans by a particular community to enter the government machinery. Behind all this, it seems that a deep conspiracy with a long-term goal is working. On the strength of numbers, preparations are being made to adopt any route to get their points convinced.'[11]

In this case, we find a different and more dangerous version of Muslim-politicophobia. The report not only remains critical to the protests led by Muslims in different parts of the country. It goes one step further to target even those educated Muslims, who follow the established procedure and constitutional mechanism as citizens to participate in public life.

---

11. For details, see 'Report of the Rashtriya Swayamsevak Sangh's Akhil Bharatiya Pratinidhi Sabha'. *Karnavati*, 13 March, 2022, p. 40.

Hijab and the Hindutva Constitutionalism

This brings us to our second question, the nature of secularism in the hijab controversy. The Government Order issued on 5 February 2022 actually was the first legal move by the government to provide validity to the hijab-ban practice followed by the educational institutions in Udupi. This order invoked the Karnataka Education Act 1983 to justify the powers of the government to endorse uniform policy. Underlining the need to have social harmony and uniformity, it envisages the hijab as a threat to equality, unity, and public order. The Order says:

'As the Supreme Court and various High Courts have held that restricting students from coming to school wearing head scarfs or head covering is not in violation of Article 25 of the Constitution, and after carefully examining the rules under Karnataka Education Act 1983...we direct students of all government schools to wear the uniform fixed by the state... In colleges that fall under the Karnataka Board of Pre-University Education, dress code prescribed by the College Development Committee... must be followed. If the administration does not fix a dress code, *clothes that do not threaten equality, unity, and public order must be worn.*'[12]

It is important to note that the Karnataka Education Act 1983 does not have any direct provision for school uniform policy. Section 7 of this Act empowers the government to issue circulars with regard to curricula, syllabi, textbooks and other practical management related issues. It also offers a long list of objectives that includes the preservation of the rich heritage of our composite culture and dignity of women. The Government Order, however, reads this list of

---

12. (emphasis mine); see https://www.scobserver.in/journal/karnataka-government-order-on-dress-code-for-students/

objectives rather mechanically. Invoking the powers given to the state government under Section 133(2) of this Act to impose a rigid uniform law.[13]

The High Court judgement redefines this mechanical reading of law as a form of positive secularism… Government Order…does not prescribe any uniform but only provides for prescription in a structured way, which we have already upheld in the light of our specific finding that wearing hijab is not an essential religious practice and school uniform to its exclusion can be prescribed. It hardly needs to be stated that the uniform can exclude any other apparel like bhagwa or blue shawl that may have the visible religious overtones.[14]

The court focuses on a highly debatable legal doctrine, the test of essential religious practices, to determine the religious significance of a particular collective act with regard to secular values. On the other hand, it justifies the rigid official interpretation of the existing laws. The court finds the exclusion of hijab and/or any other apparel symbolic of religion as 'a step forward in the direction of emancipation and to the access to education.' This attitude is defined as positive secularism.[15]

This notion of secularism contributes to what I call Hindutva Constitutionalism. I have argued elsewhere that constitutionalism should not entirely be understood as a

---

13. Section 133 (2) of the Karnataka Education Act, 1983 says: 'The State Government may give such directions to any educational institution or tutorial institution as in its opinion are necessary or expedient for carrying out the purposes of this Act.'

14. W.P. NO.2347 OF 2022/ 15 March 2022 pp.117.

15. For an excellent criticism of this kind of secularism, see Bhargava, Rajeev. 'What is Secularism For?'. *Secularism and Its Critics*, edited by Rajeev Bhargava, OUP, 1998, pp. 466-582.

normative concept that seeks to impose certain limits and curbs on the state institutions. The political actors, parties and groups, however, do not always follow this normative ideal. They interpret the provisions of the Constitution very differently to produce various ideologically suitable interpretations. The Hindutva constitutionalism is one such political form.[16] The Hindutva groups, like other political formations, engage with the Constitution to nurture their ideological agenda.

The adherence to the mechanical interpretation of law and the constitutional discourse is one of the core features of Hindutva constitutionalism. The Hindutva groups make an important distinction between the principles of the Constitution and the legal technicalities and exceptions. The principles and high moral ideals enshrined in the Constitution are invoked as settled issues. While the legal technicalities are seen as unfinished business.[17] This principles-technicalities binary helps the Hindutva groups, especially the BJP, to appropriate even those concepts and ideas that do not fit in their ideological framework. The attitude of the BJP leaders in the Hijab debate underlines the practical manifestation of Hindutva constitutionalism. The Government Order ignored the principles on which the Karnataka Education Act 1983 is based. Instead,

---

16. See Ahmed, Hilal. 'New India, Hindutva Constitutionalism, and Muslim Political Attitudes.' Studies in Indian Politics, Vol.10, no.1, 2022, pp.62-78.

17. RSS head Mohan Bhagwat says: 'Our constitution [is]... based on the understanding of the "bharatiya" ethos of our founding fathers, but many of the laws that we are still using are based on the foreign sources and that laws were made as per their thinking...seven decades have passed since our independence...this is something we must address.' See https://www.firstpost.com/india/rss-chief-mohan-bhagwat-says-there-is-need-to-develop-legal-system-based-on-ethos-of-society-4029775.html

technicalities associated with school uniform policy is taken as a point of departure to create an environment where Hijab will always be understood as a violation of law.

Let me conclude by highlighting the placing of the hijab debate in the contemporary Hindutva project. The discovery of Hijab as a form of potential political issue underlines the fact that Hindutva politics is deeply obsessed with Muslim politicophobia. In fact, the success of Hindutva lies in its enthusiastic search for those issues that might sustain Hindu-Muslim antagonism. Hindutva politics, nevertheless, is not based on any intelligible set of ideological principles. There is certainly a reservoir of floating ideas—Indianization, Hindu pride, cultural nationalism, Rashtriya Suraksha, Swadeshi and so on—that have evolved over the years. These ideas, however, are never placed in any coherent structure. This openness and non-conformity allow the Hindutva groups to take context-appropriate positions. The Hindutva constitutionalism empowers them to offer a legal justification to this ideological fuzziness.

The search for coherence in Hindutva politics is futile. Instead, there is a need to pay close attention to the ways in which a set of conflicting claims are strategically organized to interpret the everydayness of social life as civilizational clashes. Such a possible line of inquiry might help us to understand the reason why a slogan like Beti Bachao Beti Padhao (protect girls, educate girls) continues to survive in an environment where Hijab wearing girl students are not allowed to sit in a classroom.

PART TWO

READING
THE BAN

OF TOLERANCE AND TOLERATION
Thinking Through Hijab and Beef Ban

Tanweer Fazal

In the raging debate over the right to adorn hijab by girl students of a pre-university college in Karnataka, what is often missed out is the whole idea of tolerance. For a multi-ethnic polity such as India, tolerance is the foundational canon, the negation of which renders the democratic ideal vacuous and meaningless. Minimally, tolerance would imply enduring an item or a practice irrespective of the abhorrence that it may engender. A 'no harm test' is usually the guiding principle. The principle, proposed by the father of English liberalism, J.S. Mill, is designed to restrict state encroachment on personal liberty. It holds that a 'social disapproval or dislike' for the actions of an individual (or a set of individuals) does not provide sufficient ground for state intervention unless they actually cause harm or are potentially harmful to others.

A non-adherence to the principle of "no harm" in restricting harmless practices would border on coercion. A truly expansive idea of tolerance would entail that the concept of harm is most narrowly defined. Very often states limit tolerance of practices and beliefs on the plea of a speculative harm to "public order." But even an elementary doctrine of tolerance pre-requisites that the collapse of public order is explained in terms of concrete harm that the belief system, sexual orientation, dietary preference, occupational choice or customary practice has caused—not hearsay or conjecture alluding to it. Thus, in a society where heteronormativity prevails, the plea of maintaining public order to proscribe heterosexual inclinations is certainly not defensible. It goes without saying that for a tolerant society and polity, it is both prudent and desirable that before proscribing a practice, it undertakes cost-benefit analysis, and evaluates whether the objections raised against the given practice are genuine and scrupulous. These caveats are necessary for a just resolution of competing contentions.

Tolerance and Toleration

It is all the more important to distinguish the old idea of tolerance from the modern concept of toleration—the former could be misconstrued as an act of benevolence or patronage, while the latter enters the domain of equal rights and entitlements. The Parsi *qissa* that the local King of Sanjan (Gujarat), Jadi Rana granted asylum to the refuge-seeking Zoarastrians while conditionally granting them permission to observe their faith in private could be termed an act of tolerance or magnanimity of the King. Similarly, in the much-feted millet system of the Ottoman Turks, religious freedom and cultural autonomy in the form of personal laws was assured to the *dhimmies* or the religious minorities—this did not however extend to the right of holding political offices. The Mauryan King Ashoka's edict introduced the principle of harm along with the idea of religious freedom—that both, praise of one's own sect and criticism of other's should be moderate. The idea of tolerance prevailed in the past too, but was inherently limited, restricted chiefly to matters of faith and conviction. Besides, equality of individuals, irrespective of faith in matters temporal or secular, was still a far cry.

Tolerance is a value, a matter of personal orientation and moral make-up. Toleration, on the other, is a constitutional principle, part of statecraft and legal order. However, there is an intrinsic relationship between the two. For toleration to be effective, a tolerant society is a pre-requisite. Electoral democracies owing to the tyranny of numbers could potentially turn majoritarian, if not built on the scaffold of toleration. In that sense, toleration is inevitably tied to the process of democratization. Van Der Burg, drawing from the Dutch experience, examines tolerance as a normative principle for political and legal institutions. The Dutch tradition of tolerance was guaranteed in the Union of Utrecht (1579) that marked the inauguration of the Dutch republic. Religious tolerance was underlined as freedom of conscience and freedom to hold religious ceremonies in private. However, it was a limited tolerance as Protestant dissidents and Catholics were denied equal rights in contrast to the members of the Dutch Reformed Church. Tolerance was restricted to religious belief. About a century later, the sphere of tolerance was expanded to political ideas and free press so long as it did not distress public order. It legalized civil disobedience and upheld conscientious objection of minority groups to military service. The practice of tolerance was further broadened to delink it from public order altogether. But the Dutch idea of tolerance had its flip-side too. It rested on a compartmentalized society with the Protestants, the Catholics, the Liberals and Social Democrats being its four constitutive pillars each with its own schools, hospitals, even newspapers, radio and television channels which extends to separate grocery shops. Live and let live amounted to living together separately.[1]

The Indian situation is radically different. It is not separateness but inter-dependence that defines the social make-up. The local economy that has evolved organically further attests to it. Thus, a Qureshi meat-seller is a supplier of meat to both Hindus and Muslims, the castes associated with scavenging are expected to extended their services to households of all faiths and confessions, so does a weaver who is predominantly a Muslim. The Chhipa Muslims in Rajasthan excel in fabric printing while the Mahajans who make most of the profit are the Marwaris and Hindu Banias. In fact, to heuristically conceptualize a Hindu, Muslim or a Christian society insulated from each other is unfathomable. This mutuality has its own shortcomings. A well-entrenched social hierarchy reinforces the interdependent relationship between social groups, castes and communities. Tolerance draws its meaning and essence from such a complex nature of social formation in India wherein it could imply tolerating most inhuman and demeaning customs and practices. From the old idea of tolerance, it is therefore important to move to the modern concept of toleration—an elaborate system of justiciable rights and guarantees.

The modern Indian Constitution surpasses the limited nature of tolerance, and comes around to uphold the

---

1. Burg, Wibren Van Der. 'Beliefs, Persons and Practices: Beyond Tolerance'. *Ethical Theory and Moral Practice*, Vol. 1, No. 2, Jun., 1998, pp. 227-254.

principle of toleration. It proscribes potentially harmful and demeaning practices such as Sati and "untouchability" in all its forms. It enshrines freedom of conscience and the right to 'profess and propagate' religions of their choice. It is the individual who is the bearer of these inviolable rights and not communities or groups. This would imply that the individuals also have the right to exit from a particular religious form or seek reforms and alterations within. Public order, morality and health are the limiting conditions that constrain the intemperate invocation of religious freedom.[2] In a complex polity such as ours, both the interpretation of this freedom and of the limiting conditions necessitate extreme caution or else it could invite two mutually opposed accusations—majoritarian imposition or minority appeasement.

Objections to Hijab

There are several objections to the hijab or the head scarf. The most vociferous and thereby the most visible is the one voiced by the Hindutva activists. The crux of the argument rests on uniformity—from sameness in dress and costumes to uniform civil code, the range is wide. Universality here is conflated with uniformity. The cultural artifacts of this uniformity are invariably drawn from purported norms, beliefs and practices of the dominant culture. In India, though Islam and Muslims have been the objects of hate, the argument is also used to admonish Valentine's Day celebrations, women wearing western dress, deleting portions from school textbooks to protesting against dress codes in catholic schools. Clearly a supremacist position,

2. Article 25, Constitution of India.

it is incompatible with the most elementary principle of tolerance.

The second kind of objection is advanced by a section of secular-modernists for whom traditional customs and practices per se are "devil incarnates" and their public visibility repugnant to liberal values and taste. Feminists subscribing to this "difference-blind approach" have supported hijab ban or refused to lend support to the anti-ban protests on the plea that hijab is a symbol of enslavement, and clearly not an emblem of liberation. The doctrine of choice that liberal feminists often flag in matters of dress, profession, choice of partners or sexual orientation to counter hegemonic gender discourses is abandoned in this case. Hijab is socially conditioned, runs the argument. Mill's liberal philosophy had no room for such prescriptions; 'the only purpose for which power can be rightfully exercised over any member of a civilized community, against his will, is to prevent harm to others. His own good, either physical or moral, is not a sufficient warrant'[3](quoted in Epstein 378). Further, underlying this feminist position is the idea that the path to modernity and liberty is singular and pre-ordained. That free will is free only to the extent that it pursues prescribed means and goals.

There is another set of argument that rests on pedagogical practices arguing that uniforms are the prerogative of the schools and the purpose behind them is to obviate distinctions of income groups among pupils attending the same school. However, the internal logic of this argument is difficult to sustain when the class distinctions today

---

3. See Epstein, Richard A. 'The Harm Principle—And How It Grew'. *The University of Toronto Law Journal*, Vol. 45, No. 4, Autumn, 1995, pp. 369-417.

emerge from the structurally-imposed choice of the schools itself, than with the kind of dress that the student wears. The education system that has been allowed to flourish in the country structurally reproduces inequality rather than mitigating it. A superficial exercise such as sameness of the costume is of little help in this case. Besides, the proponents of hijab or turban do not make their case against the uniform as such, but for an adjustment with it. A larger argument would go deeper into the decisions to impose a particular form of dress as uniform—how is the decision made, what considerations prevail, are local preferences and diversity of student population taken into account before arriving at decisions to impose a uniform.

And then there are exegetical struggles over religion, texts and ethics and codes prescribed by the faith. While one set—purportedly the progressives—argues that hijab is not an Islamic practice at all, and that textual injunction is only for modest dressing, the votaries for hijab argue that their religion binds them to it. The trouble is that these are not merely internal interpretive contestations of the faithful over their religion but that modern courts are invariably mobilized. And what the courts have done, from the *Shirur Mutt* to the *Anand Margi* case, is to extend legal protection to only those practices *they* deem to be *essential* to that religion. Legally therefore, the hijab can only be saved if it is framed squarely within the essential practice paradigm—a move which may render a very monochromatic view of the religion itself. Religion as practiced is far closer to the everyday world of people than the scriptural versions reinforced by the courts, and it evolves and changes constantly in response to the world in which the believers live. This is a thorny terrain and renders courts into quasi-theologians. What it also does is to expel, or marginalize questions of choice and agency of practitioners.

No Harm: Hijab versus the Beef Ban

The question of hijab raised by the Muslim girls of Karnataka is evidently a complicated one. It rakes up a larger debate about uniformity versus universality, women's liberation and right to choose versus their enslavement, secularism—whether difference-blind or multi-cultural and so on. This is a question that "homogenous" nation-states of Western Europe have been grappling with for long. Assimilative policies in France forbid wearing of niqab (veil covering the face), the burkini (full body swimming costume) and hijab by girls below 18 in public spaces. Anti-separatism, equality among sexes and *laicite* or French principle of separation between Church and State are frequently invoked to validate these measures. Even though the new laws trump women's choice under the weight of such laudatory national principles, their association with the rather sordid history of French colonialism can hardly be missed in critical analysis. In contrast, the question of identity in India appeared far more settled despite occasional flare-ups. The Constitution affirms to secularism, but unlike the French doctrine, it is not the ideological vehicle to road roll homogeneity and flatten out diversity. On the contrary, the Constituent Assembly overruled amendments moved to proscribe individuals from adorning "visible signs," "mark," "name" or "dress" identified with particular religions. Krishnaswami Bharathi, member of the Constituent Assembly, intervened on the debate over whether right to propagate religion was in consonance with the principle of secularism.

> ...I(i)t is not at all inconsistent with the secular nature of the State. ...Religion will be there. ...State as such does not side with one religion or another. It tolerates all religions. Its citizens have their own religion and its communities have their own religions. It is very necessary that we should show tolerance. ...To say that some religious people should not do propaganda or propagate their views is to show intolerance on our part.[4]

The Karnataka High Court in fact then turns away from this history of accommodation, in the name ironically of "Constitutional secularism." Rejecting the petitioners' plea that classrooms should be reflective of social diversity as "empty rhetoric," it ruled that: 'The school regulations prescribing dress code for all the students as one homogenous class, serve constitutional secularism,' while any accommodation for hijab would, the court averred, give rise to feelings of "social-separateness", which was of course not desirable. It dismissed the possibility that hijab could fall under the rubric of reasonable accommodation through a tautology—namely, that hijab would violate the sanctity of the uniform, failing to see that accommodations must be made precisely for cases that depart from the norm.

The high court had already chosen to elide the discriminatory nature of the government order which singularly targeted the hijabi girls by restraining alongside them their hecklers and tormentors from wearing saffron scarves. What we are witnessing thus is also the drawing of equivalence between those who wish to articulate their dearly held consciences on their bodies and persons, and those who violently wish to erase that insignia from the

---

4. Constituent Assembly Debates on 6 December 1948 Part I (volume VII) https://indiankanoon.org/doc/1933556/

public domain—in the name of maintaining public order, restoring normalcy etc.

The doctrine of toleration offers a guide to a durable resolution to such thorny question of our times. Do we permit a practice that is adhered to by a section of the society? The "no harm test" is critical here. It necessitates separation of "abstract harm" from "concrete harm." The former derives from conjectures, speculations, predominant assumptions or utopian ideas of emancipation, in contrast, the latter is evidently injurious to the individual or group. Does the wearing of hijab in schools and universities, in public offices, commercial places—in public or in private— cause material or bodily harm to any individual or group, including the one adhering to such a practice? Palpably, the answer is no. Wearing hijab or habit, sporting a beard, having a turban or a skull cap offers no concrete harm. In fact, their denial could be deleterious, and adversely affect believing individual's chances of pursuing a profession, seeking education or public office.

If the ban on hijab is unsustainable within the logic of no harm, the ban on slaughter of cow and its progeny is untenable for inflicting real harm. With the ascendance of Hindutva, many state governments such as Maharashtra, Gujarat and Haryana imposed total ban on the slaughter of cow and its progeny such as bulls, bullocks, ox etc. A total ban on slaughter resulted in incalculable loss of livelihoods connected to the bovine economy. It is estimated that the Maharashtra government's decision to go for complete ban affected nearly two million people directly dependent on beef and related products. This includes innumerable number of butchers, workers in small establishments, owners of petty shops, eateries serving meat products or those who simply made their living by buying, selling and transporting cattle. Another 2.5 million, employed in the domestic hide industry, lost their livings.[5] In addition, it weakened the cattle rearing farmer's position in the domestic market. According to one estimate, within a year of the imposition of the total ban, prices of milch cows fell by more than ₹15,000 per animal and those for male calves, bulls and old cows plummeted from ₹18-19000 to ₹15-16000 per animal. The inability to sell the old animals compelled the farmers to abandon them, leading to a rise in the number of stray cattle.[6] The problem of stray cattle forced farmers in states such as Uttar Pradesh, Bihar, Maharashtra and Chhattisgarh to keep round the clock vigil to stop them from destroying standing crop.

Toleration and no harm principle work in tandem. It gives us an unyielding framework to draw the line between tolerable and intolerable in multi-ethnic democracies. This is easier said than done for there are many borderline cases, and multiple conceptualizations of "harm" itself. The stated reason for the blanket ban on slaughter is secular—promoting animal husbandry and milk production for instance, and not faith in the sacredness of the cow. It thus foresees the consumption of beef and slaughter of cattle as harmful to agricultural economy. A counter rationale however computes the innumerable human suffering that loss of livelihood could result in. Given the reasons, a total ban on cattle slaughter fails the test of "no harm". It warrants creation of alternative livelihood and dietary

---

5. Basrur, Nitin. 'Beef Ban and the Deprivation of livelihoods'. *India Resists*, 31 May 2016 https://indiaresists.com/beef-ban-deprivation-livelihoods/
6. Basrur, Nitin. 'Beef Ban and the Deprivation of livelihoods'.

options to substitute for the concrete harm inflicted by the prohibition. In the absence of such measures in place, state actions come to be perceived as one-sided, prejudicial and deleterious. In diverse and deeply divided societies, integration is a challenge. Toleration underwrites integration.

A SOVEREIGN BODY

A Visceral View on Muslim Women's Perpetual Imagination with Hijab[1]

Shirin Saeidi

The symbolic use of hijab to express solidarity with religious extremism is often cited by sovereign states as a reason for state regulation of Muslim women's dress. Yet, in my years of researching a particularly powerful Islamic movement, Hizbollah, I've not met one woman whose commitment to wearing the hijab was based on political calculations alone. Religious extremism is linked to domestic violence against Muslim women, as well as women from other faiths, including Judaism (Roded 2015). However, research on Islamic movements does not support a connection between women's veiling and politically motivated violence against the state (Saeidi, 'Women and the Islamic Republic'). Such a connection between hijab and religious extremism has long been debunked.

---

1. The notion of perpetual imagination comes from the writing of Kevin Adonis Browne (2021a, p. 11). This essay was written prior to the September 2022 protests in Iran. However, the central argument of hijab as a cultural resource for women in their pursuit of gender equality is relevant to the current situation in Iran.

I write in the wake of various attacks on Muslim women's bodies—as well as the academic responses to it—in order to argue the following: The politicization of hijab impacts Muslim women's sovereignty over their bodies most explicitly by dissuading women from practicing the skill and claiming their right to experience a full range of their own emotions. There is an emotional agility forged between the "perpetual imagination" that is activated by engaging with a cultural inheritance in real time and the freedom of a sovereign body (Browne "No Words", 11). For example, the act of putting on or taking off the material substance of hijab can bring emotions to the forefront in new ways. As a researcher, I often travel between Iran and the United States; I've developed intellectually between the fragmented spaces that nation-states produce, and experimenting with hijab has played a central part in learning to identify my emotions and recognizing my bodily sovereignty.

The scarf is a cultural resource for me. I've gained a sense of confidence when removing mandatory veils. I've learned to see beauty in the majestical self-restraint that modesty manifests. I've developed an understanding that the self-consciousness of a muhajabah (one with hijab) can be an attribute of occupying a new state of being. The personal practice, private challenges, and public observation of hijab have taught me how to sit still with different emotions in my body and to connect with my own emotions, which has become a kind of meditation that aids me in being a better writer. Indeed, there are variations of perpetual imaginations on the individual and collective level. In this essay, I focus more on the collective level.

Islamophobia and state regulation of hijab creates a societal aggression toward Muslim women that endangers and lessens the quality of their lives (Yaghoobi 2021). But I want to bring attention to other consequences of such disruptive acts and how women respond to them: These regulative measures also work to obstruct a woman's right to experience the full range of her own emotions; they prevent her from fully knowing herself. Even traditions with significant historical and cultural differences, such as Sufism and Taoism, assert that by exercising the ability to process one's emotions, we can—through inner tranquility and gradual access to the highest levels of human creativity—discover the source that sustains us (Izutsu 1983). According to widely different traditions, the state of being connected and in harmony with oneself is a notable place in the world from which peace emanates (Izutsu 1983). This state of grace is learned by identifying the different emotions one experiences and mastering the simultaneous task of remaining a sovereign body. In this piece, I want to highlight this connection between physical sovereignty, emotional knowledge, and progressive political change.

A lack of attention to how Muslim women themselves make the connections between hijab, bodily sovereignty, and visceral growth is a consistent theme in discussions due to the policy-oriented nature of research pertaining to hijab. Being grounded in a sovereign body holds significant political ramifications for Muslim women, in "knowing how to move—or daring to" with one's emotions (Browne 48). The remainder of this essay will further highlight this point by examining a case study of Iranian American contentions regarding compulsory hijab. A brief example from my recently published book can introduce this topic: I argue that after 1979, Iranian women have been at the forefront of citizenship struggles to establish gender equality (Saeidi, 'Women and the Islamic Republic'). From prison cells, to warfronts, to formal spaces for activism, Iranian women have challenged the masculinist nature of the modern Iranian state by relying on their bodies and emotions to intervene in routine forms of governance.

Fighting for Muslim women's right to choose hijab is one method for remaking—in real time—the space in which we live. The choice to veil moves beyond a discourse of demanding rights from a state. It's the prerogative of female-identifying Muslims to explore the practice of hijab. From our given and chosen ancestors we inherit different Islamic cultures, but it is the female-identifying perpetual imagination that becomes a tool for holding, making, and unmaking spaces. The practice, and even the fabric, of hijab is utilized in pursuit of gender equality.

A Perpetual Imagination of Non-Violence: Muslim Women, Feminists, and the Limits of Solidarity with Masih Alinejad's Campaigns

Among Iranians, there is nothing particularly new about the contentions surrounding compulsory hijab. For the past 170 years Iranian women have been battling the state over mandatory unveiling and re-veiling policies (Yaghoobi 2021). During the reign of Reza Shah (1923–41), a mandatory unveiling was enforced by decree, and the 1979 revolution, which established an Islamic Republic, brought forth compulsory veiling. Both enforcements targeted women's bodies and were met with significant resistance from within society. Movements against compulsory hijab develop within specific spaces and as responses to particular historical contingencies. The Iranian Diaspora has seen a large body of literature produced in the contemporary era that uses creative writing to explore the contentious legacies of hijab (Yaghoobi 2021).

The following Iranian American case is just one instance of a transnational movement against compulsory hijab that is centered on women's sovereignty over their bodies. In the process of highlighting Muslim women's struggles to maintain bodily sovereignty, the relation between emotions and political creativity is also exposed. Ultimately, I argue that this particular Iranian American experience (of claiming a sovereign body by contesting mandatory hijab) exemplifies a perpetual imagination of non-violence in the pursuit of political change. The struggle to delineate their right to bodily sovereignty has advanced the capacity of Iranian women to understand on a fundamental level the emotions that physical violation and violence can produce. However, these first-hand experiences also call attention to the significant cultural tension engendered between women as a result of forced policy.

In May 2014, Masih Alinejad, an exiled Iranian journalist living in the United Kingdom, launched a Facebook page titled 'My Stealthy Freedom.' Alinejad started a campaign to challenge the Islamic Republic of Iran's compulsory veiling policy by encouraging Iranian women in Iran to take photos of themselves in public places without the scarf (Saul 2016). Alinejad's Instagram page currently has 6.5 million followers with a significant number based in Iran. While her role as a leader of the movement against compulsory hijab in Iran remains controversial, there is no denying that Alinejad is a major figure in the transnational "cultural invasion" that the Islamic Republic has long anticipated (Shahi and Abdoh-Tabrizi 2020).

It remains unclear, however, if Alinejad positions herself

against mandatory hijab and the establishment of an Islamic Republic in Iran, or if she has gradually and unintentionally become the face of an Islamophobic movement against hijab in the United States. Her 'search for the disreputable' in Islam and among Muslims is rooted in her personal experiences with piety politics in an Islamic state (Lazreg 1988, 89). In her memoir, *The Wind in My Hair* (2018), Alinejad recounts that her father forced her to veil, even at bedtime. She recalls that he would be angered if her scarf moved and made her hair visible while she slept. Alinejad discusses numerous episodes of public shaming and violence that centered on her body at every phase during her growth from a young girl to a woman. What should have been joyful and warm emotions appropriate to experiences like childhood play, marriage, and pregnancy were often disrupted by acts of violence against Alinejad's body by men close to her and by strangers, all of whom gave themselves the right to violate her bodily sovereignty. With disrupted physical sovereignty and as a result of constantly inhabiting survival mode, Alinejad also lost the right to sense, sit with, and work through her own emotions in an organic and harmonious manner.

Compulsory veiling is one fundamental tool, among many, in the hands of patriarchs who use it to obstruct a woman's capacity to discover her own emotions through a sovereign body. For instance, Alinejad recalls telling her first husband that she was marrying him not for love but only to gain the right of physical mobility. She dreamed of living in Tehran, something she could never do as a single woman because of her family's restrictions. Alinejad's violent experiences and struggles over control of her body are ramifications of many factors, including the state institutionalization of religion. Alinejad asserts that compulsory hijab is an attack on a woman's body but that deciding to veil should be a woman's personal decision and right (Yaghoobi 2021). As such, a reckoning remains. For those of the Muslim faith, including postcolonial academics, the task remains to find constructive ways in dealing with the messy aftermath of religious extremism as it interrupts all lives in devastating ways. There is an urgency for academics concerned with modern Iran and the Iranian diaspora to shed light on the innovative healing techniques forged from within societies that have experienced extensive political violence.

Since initiating her campaign against compulsory veiling, Muslim women (including those in Iran) have repeatedly accused Alinejad of activating a militaristic discourse against the people of Iran in exchange for personal profit (Zangeneh 2019). These accusations are not completely unfounded. Alinejad took part in a series of controversial meetings with US political and media elites, including a 2019 meeting with US Secretary of State Mike Pompeo (Radio Farda 2019). Between 2015 and 2019, Alinejad received US government contract funds amounting to US$305,000 for her work at the state-owned media company Voice of America (Clifton 2020). She has also asserted that hijab is not part of Iranian culture despite the fact that Iran is an overwhelmingly Muslim majority country (Ghattas 2018).

Most recently, Alinejad has accused US Congresswoman Ilhan Omar of creating the contingencies needed to justify Islamic extremism by introducing the Combating International Islamophobia Act, a bill that passed with a house vote of 219–212 (Alinejad 2022). In a *Washington Post* article, Alinejad claims that many women's rights activists in the US are fearful to join her campaign of denouncing compulsory hijab because the label Islamophobic does not have a clear definition (Alinejad 2022). In response to Omar's legislation, Alinejad launched the #LetUSTalk hashtag on social media by which Muslim women could post photos of themselves with forced hijab in Iran compared to photos of themselves in states—often Western states—to which they had migrated.

Regarding her effort to connect with feminists after the 2017 Women's March, Alinejad states that 'Weeks after the Women's March, I reached out to some of the organizers to seek their help for my campaign against compulsory hijab. I found that hardly anyone was willing to support my campaign lest they be accused of promoting Islamophobia' (2022). Her recent *Washington Post* article suggests that she is aware of the significant distance that exists between herself and feminists in the US (Alinejad 2022). Indeed, both Muslim and feminist writers from the Middle East have critiqued tactics that center on Islamic exceptionalism. For instance, Seddighi and Tafakori acknowledge that the issue is not the obvious harm in Iran's mandatory veiling policy, rather it is the use of militarized language to undermine the law in the country's Islamic penal code that has made Alinejad the target of criticism (2016).

As such, one is led to wonder what keeps US feminists away from Alinejad's campaigns: the fear of being labeled an Islamophobic activist or the real-time outcry of secular, Muslim, and feminist activists who oppose Alinejad's political strategies. Alinejad's financial and political ties to the Trump administration made her activism problematic for other Muslim women activists. In her accusations against Omar, she joins many white women in the Republican Party who have also made derogatory claims against the only black Muslim female (and one of two Muslim American women) elected to serve in Congress (Kaczynski 2021).

While I agree with the academic and activist critiques of Alinejad's political approaches in addressing women's rights in Iran, I would like to bring attention to a lesser noted aspect of this transnational battle: the Hijab as a cultural resource used to experience a broad range of emotions, to delineate a sovereign body, and to enable participation in a perpetual imagining of gender equality. With Iranian women's rich history of activism geared toward maintaining a sovereign body, there is an urgency to understand how hijab operates as a cultural resource that reveals something about the perpetual imagination of Iranian women in this particular moment.

Women in Iran—and Muslim women elsewhere—are not critical of Alinejad because she is participating in Iranian politics from the US, or because of her seeming distrust of Islamic traditions. It is not a lack of empathy, care, or comprehension regarding the complexities of women's experiences with religious extremism that creates a distance between Alinejad and Muslim feminist activists. In other words, there is shared empathy regarding one another's experiences. Instead, it is Alinejad's political strategy of aligning with US figures and discourses, understood by many Muslim women to be violent, that limits her reach within the elite Muslim and Western activist communities with whom she wishes to connect.

Muslim women are critical of Alinejad because her support for a woman's right to choose veiling also undermines freedom by giving a platform to other forces that include practices, language, and individuals that invite violence toward Muslim women. The opposition against

Alinejad is overwhelmingly one that pursues a worldview rooted in freedom as a halt of state regulation of women's bodies. By siding with forces in the US that support war on Iran and Islamophobic viewpoints that challenge democracy in the US, Alinejad falls behind the currents and waves of Iranian women's perpetual imagination with hijab.

Exploring the Iranian American movement against compulsory hijab demonstrates that decades of fighting mandatory veiling and un-veiling among Iranians has set into motion a perpetual imagination of non-violent political change. Amidst the tension that exists between Alinejad and other Muslim and feminist activists, we see that Iranian women are already unveiling, re-veiling, and revealing their critiques of the Islamic Republic, Western hegemony, and patriarchy. As such, our view is pushed toward women's everyday struggles, the small and large wins that they reap in Iran and elsewhere. With hijab understood as a cultural resource that can be manipulated in the hands of different patriarchs, we are indeed eager to see what Iranian women are teaching us about freedom, the limits of the state, and a world without citizenry hierarchies and boundaries. The space that these women hold, unmake, and remake for freedom and peace is space for us all—in Islamic states, Western democracies, and any other organizational structure that we may experience in the future.

References

Alinejad, Masih. *The Wind in My Hair: My Fight for Freedom in Modern Iran.*
Little, Brown and Company, 2018.
___."Opinion: Why I'm Opposed to Ilhan Omar's Bill Against Islamophobia". The Washington Post, 25 January 2022.
Browne, K. A. "No Words". *Brick: A literary Journal*, vol. 106, 2021, pp. 8-18.
___."A Douen Epistemology: Caribbean Memory and the Digital Archive". *College English*, vol. 84, no. 1, pp. 33-57.
Clifton, E. 2020. "U.S. Media Outlets Fail to Disclose US Government Ties of "Iranian Journalist" Echoing Trump Talking Points". Responsible Statecraft, 6 January 2020.
Ghattas, K. "Those Who Dare to Bare Their Hair". Foreign Policy, 16 July 2018.
Izutsu, Toshihiko. *Sufism & Taoism: A Comparative Study of Key Philosophical Concepts.* U of California P. 1983.
Kaczynski, A. "Another Video Shows Lauren Boebert Suggesting Ilhan Omar Was a Terrorist". 2021. www.cnn.com/2021/11/30/politics/lauren-boebert-ilhan-omar-video-comments/index.html.
Lazreg, M. "'Feminism and Difference': The Perils of Writing as a Muslim Woman on Women in Algeria". *Feminism Studies,* vol.14, no.1, 1988, pp. 81-107.
"Pompeo Tells Iranian Rights Activist of U.S. Support". Radio Farda. 2019. http/en.radiofarda.com/a/pompeo-meets-with-alinejad-and-voices-us-support/ 29752266.html.
Roded, Ruth. "Islamic and Jewish Religious Feminists Tackle Islamic and Jewish Oral Law: Maintenance and Rebellion of Wives". *Comparative Islamic Studies*, vol. 11, no. 1, 215, pp. 35-63.
Saeidi, Shirin. "Hizbollah in Global Arena". *Oxford Research Encyclopedias.* 2022 (Forthcoming).
Saeidi, Shirin. *Women and the Islamic Republic: How Gendered Citizenship Conditions the Iranian State.* Cambridge UP, 2022.
Saul, H. "My Stealthy Freedom: Women in Iran Step Up Hijab Campaign by Filming Themselves Walking in Public With Their Heads Uncovered". 2016. See https://www.independent.co.uk/news/world/middle-east/my-stealthy-freedom-women-in-iran-step-up-hijab-campaign-by-filming-themselves-walking-in-public-10149226.html.

Seddighi, Gilda and Sara Tafakori. "Transnational Mediation of State Gendered Violence: The Case of Iran". *Feminist Media Studies*, vol. 16, no. 5, pp. 925–928.

Shahi, A and E Abdoh-Tabrizi. "Iran's 2019-2020 Demonstrations: The Changing Dynamics of Political Protests in Iran". *Asian Affairs*, vol. 51, no. 1. 2020. pp. 1-41.

Yaghoobi, C. "Over Forty Years of Resisting Compulsory Veiling: Relating Literary Narratives to Text-Based Protests and Cyberactivism". *Journal of Middle East Women's Studies*, vol. 17, no. 2, 2021. pp. 220-239.

Zangeneh, N. "Against Opportunist Feminism, Masih Alinejad and Her Apostles". 2019. See, https://pecritique.files.wordpress.com/2019/02/against-opportunist-feminism.pdf.

HIJABING, RE-HIJABING, DE-HIJABING

Women in Scarves and 'Triple Humiliation' in Post-Mandal India

P.K. Yasser Arafath

Over the last few years, the debates over the complexity
of gender relations within Islamic societies have generated
a range of arguments about the hijab (head scarf), and its
complex relations with Muslim women. Hijab, like any
sartorial marking, gets new meanings every now and then,
depending on the changing political and social contexts.
However, it continues to carry the residues of Eurocentric
interpretation of it as an instrument of oppression across
time and space. Equally, a section of non-Muslim liberals
view it as a discardable irritation while Hindutva politics
identifies it as an Islamist sign of non-allegiance with the
"nation." However, early Muslim feminist scholars have
argued against such fixed, orientalist, liberal, and neo-
nationalist espousals on hijab since the last quarter of
the 20th century. New feminist research examines the
constantly changing meanings of hijab, looking at how
young, educated, and working Muslim women adopt hijab

to achieve certain kinds of moral and pietistic authority, political voice, and autonomy in the post-modern world.

The hijab debate is back again after a group of right-wing vigilantes harassed hijab wearing Muslim students in a college in Karnataka. The visuals of such groups and their chasing girls with head scarves in few other colleges have created a huge uproar across the world. World's influential intellectuals like Noam Chomsky have expressed deep concerns, considering such incidents as a reflection of rising Islamophobic vigilantism in India today. In her twitter message, Nobel laureate Malala Yusufzai stated that 'refusing to let girls go to school in their hijabs is horrifying. Objectification of women persists—for wearing less or more. Indian leaders must stop the marginalisation of Muslim women.' Reference Vigilante groups' attacks on the "deviant" cultural markers, especially Islamic ones, have increased across the state, especially after the recently concluded urban local body elections in which the BJP received a massive set back in the hands of the Congress party. They are wasting no time, with tacit or open support from their extended kinship, to continuously insinuate secularphobic narratives, challenging the very foundation of Constitutional rights of citizens.

Multivalent Scarves

The hijab has a very long history, and Muslim women have covered their head in a variety of different ways in the past. It has elicited a variety of reactions from non-Muslim observers and Muslim intellectuals and religious scholars from time to time. In fact, an organized smear campaign against such Muslim sartorial markers may be traced back to the early orientalist writers who began to intensively observe Muslim households and social engagements in the 19th century. According to Edward Said, Muslim women wearing the "veil" (head and facial covering) had been a prominent target in Orientalist literary discourses, and the "veil" had come to symbolize Muslim sexual fantasy, Islam's deep secret, and rigidity.[1] Like its physical plurality, headscarves have evoked different meanings across cultures and political times. In short, hijab has no fixed meaning. Quite a few Muslim women scholars, including Lila Abu Lughod, Amina Wadud, Fatima Mernissi, and Saba Mahmood, have explained various reasons as to why urbane and educated Muslim women from various ethno-cultural regions resorted to wearing the hijab from the last quarter of the 20th century. Modern head covering among educated Muslim women originated as a political movement against various power structures in the Arab world in the late 1970s, according to Abu Lughod, one of the world's major anthropologists. In 2016, I conducted an ethnographic study in Kerala on this topic, which revealed the sociological, cultural, economic, material, bodily, security, aesthetic, pietistic, and identitarian aspects that Muslim women used to negotiate with hijab and purdah (covering coat).

Today, the headscarf is acquiring a complex meaning in India, where young Muslim women—educated, English-speaking, and urbane—have begun to see it as a conduit of dissent and resentment, echoing what one saw in the Arab Islamic world in the late 1970s, when the bodies of Muslim women became the site of political and ideological contestations. As a result, putting the hijabi Muslim woman into the predictable "oppression-liberation" binary erases many of the implications she carries in the ever-

---

1. See Said, Edward. *Orientalism*. Penguin Books, 2003, p.190.

changing Islamophobic neoliberal environment. As Muslims cease to exist as a "concrete community" they undergo constant motion across the globalized world. Thus, they are not different from any other community whose identity formation and sense of allegiance gets complicated due to continuous motion and mobility in a changing world. Their physical mobility leads them to a different stage of emotional, material, intellectual and cognitive motion as well. These multiple mobilities are enabling a segment of Muslim women to be unconventional in their pursuits of education and employment. In the process, a good number of them have begun to consider sartorial markers such as headscarves as a stabilizer of their legitimate identity as "Muslim," and use them as counter-signification against the pervasive stereotype of clothing styles identified with Islam as instruments of oppression.

Apart from the critique of "covering" as an exclusionary act by Muslim women themselves, the post-partition Muslim woman disdained headscarf in public places for the fear of exclusion and "othering" as well. However, educated Muslim women in post-Mandal India do not seem to harbour such anxieties. The post-Mandal women in scarves seem to have the political conviction to change mainstream perceptions by integrating secular and democratic ideas with their pietistic and sartorial choices, like scholars like Sama Abdurraqib have pointed out in the case of Muslim women in the American diaspora. As the hijab takes on new meanings, urbane and educated Muslim women appear to be carving out a legitimate democratic place for themselves within the confines of the constitution while remaining unapologetic about their cultural identity. This explains why, in a neoliberal world where Islamophobia is on the rise, a huge number of second-generation post-Mandal

Muslim women are wearing hijab, when their predecessors were largely apprehensive of wearing them at colleges and universities in previous decades. Thus, the headscarves have different significance for Neo-Hijabi women than the pietistic and cultural ones, as they become a site of symbolic, political and intellectual warfare between several claimants.

The Karnataka hijab controversy exemplifies a vicious and protracted battle between male-centric religious nationalisms and Muslim women's bodies across regions. Re-hijabing and jilbabing defined the violent phase of Taliban rule in Afghanistan in the 1980s and the Islamic Republic of Iran under Ayatollah Khomeini, whereas de-hijabing—the tearing of women's sartorial markings—became a major political act in Iran under Reza Shah in the early 1920s. Even though thousands of Muslim women challenged Iran's imposition of hijab in 1979, all of them were put down by doctrine and punishment.[2] In the late 1970s, Muslim women in Tehran were broadly divided into three categories: non-hijabi, "bad hijabi," and good hijabi, with only the latter being allowed to enter the theocratic state's moral template. When it comes to open threats against hijab-wearing women in Karnataka, only non-hijabi Muslim subjects are considered as the uncontested Muslim subjects under Hindutva rule in the state. All of these examples convey the same story: Muslim women's bodies are still a site of political and ideological contestation in the modern world. When one considers the recent street protests in India that began with Shaheen Bagh in Delhi where a huge number of Muslim women were active participants, it is clear that they are no longer satisfied with being mere bearers of

---

2. See Bayat, Asef. *Life as Politics, How ordinary people change the Middle east*. Stanford UP, 2010. p.89. He explains the category 'bad hijabi' who were sentenced to short term jail terms. p. 92.

community symbols and Islamic principles. Despite this, the liberal intelligentsia, which is still locked in the out-of-dated category of "Islamic/Muslim backwardness," has disregarded their resurrected consciousness as agents of resistance and collective secular resilience.

Along with the multiple mobilities in the past two decades, educated Muslim women's increasing familiarity with hijab discourses in contested cultural and ethnic sites across the world also played a crucial role in making them believe in themselves as agents of change, of self and others. However, their sartorial assertion can only be fully explained along with the shifts in the Indian social and political landscape in the last few years. This period has witnessed a "great divide" in various interactive spaces. Muslim women's insistence on a new sartorial identity, thus, cannot also be removed from the new interactional, emotional, material and political circumstances that emerged out of this "great divide." Living consciously in the everydayness of an alienating cultural hegemony that pushes them away through subterfuge, the headscarf is turning out to be a conduit for solidarity, kinship, and self-care in India's shrinking public spaces. Amina Wadud, the eminent Muslim feminist scholar who challenged the male centric interpretation of Islam, identified a reverse sartorial shift when Muslim women became the target of 'white American radicalism' after the attack on the World Trade Center. Muslim Women were forced to hide their hijab, and their Muslim identity, and Wadud sees such forced acts as the 'erasure of being Muslim.'[3]

A rising number of progressives and a section of the

<hr>

3. See Wadud, Amina. 'Erasures: The Events of September 11th Changed Our World Forever.' *Azizah*, vol. 110, Summer 2002

Muslim intelligentsia agree that the headscarf may be used to voice effective dissent in the increasingly Islamophobic world, while another continues to make hard criticism of the tradition of veiling (Niqab) and covering (Purdah). For the former, sartorial assertion has become the most effective and non-violent conduit of dissent and subversion in the wake of the all-encompassing cultural nationalisms across the world. Therefore, the focal point of the girls in scarves in Karnataka or elsewhere needs to be transferred from the framework of 'right to education' to a more appropriate theoretical premise- the 'right to dissent'—in the most difficult political time in the history of independent India.

When bigotry has become the norm in the south Karnataka areas, as well as many other regions of India, young Muslim women appear to perceive new clothing choices as powerful instruments of dissent, confidence, and, maybe, a corporeal shield against Hindutva male vigilantes with saffron shawls, a common sight across the state of Karnataka, today. Even though the physical shield makes them an easy target for the same group that attacks the Hijabi women by howling and hooting at them, they continue to wear them. Thinking from these news contexts, 'religiosity and backwardness' would look like an obsolete framework to locate the increasing number of neo-hijabi women from amongst the post-Mandal Muslim women in colleges and universities across India. These need to be analysed along with the factors of assertion, autonomy, social mobility, political consciousness, constitutional literacy, apart from the elements of piety. Muslim women's demand for a multicultural space, their increasing involvement in the political landscape and the question of 'what it means to be a Muslim' in a culturally contested India have been three major catalysts in their rise of the neo-hijabi women for a few years now.

De-marked Body

The increasing assertion of young Muslim women wearing hijab, or head scarf, in public places has sparked a lot of discussion among Muslim intellectuals, both women and men. The hijab-centric discussions are more heated and contentious in places where Islam is still treated as a foreign religion and Muslims as aliens. The dominant argument coming from such regions look at Islam as a culture from which the oppressed women are to be liberated. Following the enunciative tools of early missionary orientalists, literary figures, and ethnographers in French and British imperial colonies that include India, Middle East, and Africa, the west still sees hijab as a mere reflection of religious oppression and Muslim sexual fetishism. However, new research from Muslim majority regions show that a large majority of Muslim women do not wear hijab due to religious pressure, patriarchal coercion, or Muslim men's sexual desires. Religious piety is only one of the reasons, and we see substantial shifts in hijab rationales among the Muslim migrant communities in Europe and America and also the post-Mandal neo-Hijabi Muslim women in India. These rationales have never been static or consistent—rather they continue to evolve. All of this does not negate the prospect of internal pressure or enforcement by certain steadfastly conservative individuals or organisations within the Muslim community.

However, when it comes to their personal choice, social autonomy, and corporeal sovereignty, the new women in scarves also reject theological codes and puritanic containers.

A growing number of Muslim women wear hijab in defiance of their unsupportive parents, who were once part of the country's more palatable political past. For them, pietistic submission to God, adhesion to a secular constitution, democratic expression of dissent, and the reclamation of public spaces have all become an organic continuum of their being Indian citizens and Muslim. One does not confront the other in such a coterminous existence. Then, why is the hijab a problem now? This takes us to the larger question of how majoritarian cultural nationalism looks at minority sartoriality and corporeality. Violent protests for de-hijabing, from the US to India, reiterate the substratum of cultural nationalisms in the contemporary world in which religious minorities are made to accept exogenous ascriptions from people and parties in power. It wants to unmark the body of cultural minorities. In any case, the visuals of a critical mass of educated women with their own sartorial choices and body markers in public places challenges the far-right vigilantes in India who cannot stomach anything beyond the tripartite matrix of assent, obedience and silence, when it comes to women, irrespective of their religions. The only difference is that they seem to be left with no human conscience when it comes to the sartorial and corporeal significations that are even remotely Islamic.

By portraying themselves as self-assured, agential, and sovereign individuals who do not want to be perceived as victims of patriarchal families and retrogressive theologians, post-Mandal neo-hijabi women challenge the stereotype of Muslims as a retarded group. Thus, the new phenomenon of Hijab wearing must be viewed as an organic response to an oppressive politics that seeks to destroy the wearer as well as the socio-psychological balance of India's already wretched Muslims. Like Fanon argues with regard to colonial Algeria, neo-hijabi women recognise that when a Hindutva vigilante encounters her, she challenges his arrogance with her hidden body. She keeps her face away from him, he is frustrated and his aggression reaches its peak, she looks permanently un-submissive, and all of it challenges his toxic politics, and powerful patrons. Then they resort to cyber de-hijabing as has been happening recently. The whole process of cyber auctioning of Muslim women is a response to their permanent un-submissiveness to masculine Hindutva violence. Thus, by tearing what they wear, this fringe could create a temporary gratification and sense of triumph.

The rape threats that hijabi/non-hijabi women frequently encounter in the cyber world reflects the extreme desperation of the aggravated Hindutva millennials who are made to believe that unveiling Muslim women is their masculine right while neo-hijabi women are increasingly convinced that wearing the hijab is their constitutional prerogative. Cyber auctioning, imaginative/real/threat of tearing of the sartorial wear is tantamount to what Fanon said, 'the double deflowering' of the Muslim womon in the continuously spiking Islamophobic atmosphere in India.[4] From the speeches and discussions immediately after reading down Article 370, in which the "fair skinned" and "beautiful" Kashmiri women were sexualized[5], to Sulli deals[6], and

4. See Fanon, Frantz, 'Algeria Unveiled'. *Decolonization: Perspectives from Now and Then*, edited by Prasenjit Duara. Routledge, 2004. p.49.

5. See 'BJP Workers Excited to Marry Fair Girls From Kashmir, Says UP MLA', *The Wire*. New Delhi. 7 Aug 2019. BJP Workers Excited to Marry Fair Girls From Kashmir, Says UP MLA (thewire.in)

6. Sulli Deals: The Indian Muslim women 'up for sale' on an app—BBC News

to the open threat of tearing the hijab in Karnataka and other parts of India, one understands the masculine and sexual insecurities that indoctrinated Hindutva millennials face when confronted with non-submissive Muslim women in public spaces that include educational institutes. These public sights of being hidden, and being untamable can unsettle, to a great extent, their sexual-psychological balance and sense of normalcy.

There is a long history of sexualizing women, and systematic sexual violence against women from religious and racial minority groups under a repressive majoritarian regime.[7] New developments around the hijab demonstrate a long-term effort to portray Muslim women as "exotic" while denying them the right to wear what they choose. Her sartorial choices trouble Hindutva's belligerent eyes. Thus, the sustained propaganda to unveil and sporadic success can also be read as an allegorical act of rape that entails the disclosure and total submission of their bodies, corporeal rights and sexual preferences. Post-Mandal Muslim women understood this more than anyone else did. Aggressive and divisive polemics against the hijab across the world clearly gave a new life to this "dead" sartorial insignia from the 19th century. In many forms, it was a part of Muslim women's everyday lives for centuries in the most docile way.

Hijab was a normal and non-controversial sartorial marker in India as well for a long time like in most of the Muslim societies as it was stabilised, without any revolutionary change in 'form or colour,' until they came into contact with colonialism.[8] However, veiling and unveiling

---

7. Saidel Rochelle G. and Sonja Maria Hedgepeth, *Sexual Violence Against Jewish Women During the Holocaust*. Brandeis UP, 2010.

8. See Fanon, op cit, p.50

have evolved as a form of protest among educated Muslim women in the imperial colonies since the 20th century. Many Muslim women chose not to wear it when the hyper-religious theologians aggressively pushed for it, but after two generations or more, women from the same households wanted to wear it simply to reject hyper-nationalism based on hegemonic cultural symbols.

Post-Mandal neo-hijabi women do not perceive themselves in the new circumstances as mere adjunct to the puritanical world of Muslim men; rather, they see themselves as independent individuals capable of establishing their own discourse and praxis. They go from being objectified as submissive to being the agents of change on their own when Hindutva politics tries to establish a permanent spectrum of triple humiliation for them being women, Muslims, and hijabi. As a result, the rejection of this politics has taken a new turn, and now the hijab is being used as an instrument of resistance. If the state or a hegemonic party harasses Muslim women for donning hijab, they respond by wearing even more of it, following a common behavioral pattern among the "wretched" communities around the world. The anti-colonial political philosopher Frantz Fanon has shown such behaviour among the colonised blacks in Algeria. When the blacks were tortured and attacked by the colonisers for being black, they did not react as passive Algerians but as active blacks, and became the victims of rigorous exclusion. Similarly in India, where Muslim women's access to education is still appalling and social mobility chances are dwindling outside of few southern states like Kerala, the persistent tearing off, and polemics regarding the hijab may ultimately hasten the process of Muslim ghettoization.

Scars, Scarves, and Scares

How do hijabi women navigate the shifting cultural landscape? A woman wearing a hijab is quickly identified and judged. For the unfamiliar, she is enigmatic and frequently acts alone! She is constantly being watched, if not stalked. She gives off the impression of being conservative, strange, reclusive, and docile. A hijabi woman goes through the corridors of public life and is required to readjust her body, her gestures, voice, and often friendship. She is in constant conflict with her past, present, her surroundings, known and unknown, intimacy, and hegemonic sartoriality. Her new invention of the body is overtly political and the object of curiosity in the Hindutva muscular matrix. Often triple humiliated in an Islamophobic world, she has to build three spaces: one in the men's world, a space within the women's world, and a new space among the non-hijabi Muslim women. The post-Mandal neo-hijabi women aim to change this by redefining what the hijab means—from a restrictive tool of subjugation to one that empowers them. She now conceives herself to be the bridge to a new future—a future with scars left behind, scarf on the head, fears set aside, democracy in thoughts and pen in hand.

It transforms, or ought to transform, the open-minded onlookers too. Now, the public visibility of neo-hijabi women in India is taken as their transformation from being the vanguard of the family and orthopraxy to becoming the vanguard of constitutional democracy and human rights in the backdrop of rising Hindutva power. It shatters the un-teachable vigilantes. As a result, the political hegemony and the religious orthodoxy are always coming up with new counter-measures to maintain their dominance and control. Theologians have historically utilised veils as a means of concealment and silence. In the past, sartorial covering and auxiliary acts ensured a predictable, and an un-transgressive Muslim woman. To the shock of Muslim ortho-praxis section, neo-hijabi women inverted the meaning and the very rationale of hijabing, and in the present it has become a window for speaking up and being seen. Thus, the new veil is used to unveil the hitherto veiled. Post-Mandal women view hijab as a conduit for subversion. Latest ethnographic studies from Indian universities show that the majority of them desire to be sovereign individuals, resilient, resistant, visible, and people with a voice—and they regard the hijab as a revolutionary enabler in the current time, making most of the earlier studies obsolete.

At a political crossroad in India, neo-hijabi women defy the values of the neoliberal political and moral order that Hindutva seeks to impose on them. It is possible that they may unveil themselves when their hegemony is diminished and the cultural context shifts, as it did in Algeria and Iran. It is also possible that more women will start donning the hijab if the political situation remains virulently polarising. For example, in Iran, many Muslim women removed their hijab when the Ulema wanted to control their lives and many resorted to it when the state wanted to remove it. In India, the doctrinal aggression of Hindutva in its design of dominance makes the post-Mandal Muslim women respond as Muslim women with their definable sartorial markers. This has created some concern within the Muslim intelligentsia that such shifts in attire can lead to a static and retrograde society.

Conclusion

In many ways, the violent shredding of the headscarf or the threats made against hijabi women show how these women are evolving into the repository of Hindutva's repressed fantasies,[9] and how the fetishization of the Hijab continues to attract youth indoctrinated by Hindutva to come onto the streets and unleash street violence in Karnataka, and other places. Similar to what occurred in colonial Algeria in the 1950s, as detailed by Fanon, the public protests also demonstrate the psycho-sexual drive of the indoctrinated millennials who wished to look beyond the faces and heads of Muslim women. The horrific effects of such imaginations have been documented in a variety of violent clashes across north India, and they continue to be one of the main draws of anti-Muslim violence in India.[10]

At the same time, the neo-hijabi women challenge the stigma associated with the sartorial Muslim in public, and the onus is placed on onlookers to change their perspective rather than they change their lives. For them the hijab is increasing its worth as a tool of resistance against the 'objectifying, humiliating, essentialising, and dehumanizing gaze at the core of religious nationalism across the world.'[11] The post-Mandal hijab is needed to create an "elsewhere" and "double outside", in order to escape from two sustainable traps—cultural nationalism and religious

9. See Silverman, Max. 'The French Republic Unveiled'. *Ethnic and Racial Studies*, vol. 30, no. 4, 2007, p. 631.

10. Parvis Ghassem-Fachandi. *Pogrom in Gujarat:Hindu Nationalism and Anti-Muslim Violence in India*, 2012, p.74.

11. See Silverman, Max. 'The French Republic Unveiled.' *Ethnic and Racial Studies*, vol.30, no.4, 2007 p. 631.

patriarchy simultaneously, like it happened elsewhere.[12]
They want to show, in some way, that they are emerging
as a voice in the post-Mandal political consciousness and
commitment. They want to stay there for a long time,
not like a contextual exigency happened as an anomaly,
and in their thoughts, hijab enables them to be invisibly
visible in public, silencing their mere body and activating
the whole body-sartorial, voice, reason, arguments, and
articulation. What disturbs the disgruntled onlookers is the
inversion of their normalcy, and the replacement of it with
a new normal, where Muslim women wearing the most
fashionable dresses paired with the hijab present themselves
as perfectly modern, thinking, individuals.

---

12. See Moore, Lindsey. 'The Veil of Nationalism: Frantz Fanon's
"Algeria Unveiled" and Gillo Pontecorvo's The Battle of Algiers.'
Kunapipi, vol.25, no. 2, 2003, p.61.

HIJAB BAN AND THE POLITICS OF CLOTHING IN CONTEMPORARY INDIA

G. Arunima

I probably belong to a tiny minority of Indians who studied in a school that didn't have a uniform. This made us feel special; it also made life simpler as one could jump into whatever was at hand and run to school. For the most part we were an ill dressed and shabby lot, but that was perhaps par for the course for those who grew up in the 1960s and 70s. Yet, I have spent a large part of my life being told by friends that having a uniform is essential and that it works as an equalizer. This is an argument that I find quite absurd, as it is patently clear that poor Indian children going to government schools wear uniforms made of very poor material whereas their wealthier counterparts going to private schools wear clothes that look stylish and almost designer made. Within schools itself, especially where the middle and upper middle classes send their children, students are marked by any number of differences. From bags, lunch boxes to other accessories like pencil cases, watches and now smart phones, the difference despite the attempt at sartorial uniformity is the reality. And such differences are just the tip of the iceberg. Interestingly enough, the Principal of our school during my years there, a Miss Sengupta, was once asked why we didn't have a uniform. Her reply, which every ex-student can recite by heart was, 'I want my students to be butterflies not soldiers.' In today's India she would have been termed an anti-national and chucked into jail for sedition.

Yet, what she said then goes to the heart of the hijab vs uniform controversy that rocked the southern Indian state of Karnataka during the months of March and April 2022. As was evident to anyone with a modicum of political intelligence, this was a row engineered by the Hindutva, or the Hindu right wing, in the Bharatiya Janta Party [henceforth, BJP] ruled state. With this, a non-issue becomes one that threatens the education of hijab-clad Muslim students in the affected educational institutions in Udupi (and in time, elsewhere). Any numbers of logical rebuttals are of no value here as this was cleverly turned into a question of upholding dress codes in schools. Additionally, with the hijab-clad students turning to the courts for legal redress, the question became not merely one of adhering to school dress code, but one of determining the very status of the hijab within Islam. The adherence to the principle of the school uniform, which until now didn't seem to have been all that inflexible—after all the same hijab-clad students had been attending school/ pre- university college until now—has now acquired the status of an inviolable law. Likewise, the hijab, with its many meanings has, in this instance, been reduced to being an ambivalent marker, which can variously be interpreted as denoting Islam's intransigence while at the same time not being "essentially Islamic" enough for it to merit protection under Indian law. The immediate provocation for such an outcome was the Muslim women students going to court, and arguing for the right to wear the hijab as the 'right to freedom of conscience' protected by Article 25 of the Indian Constitution.[1] The court's verdict, with its stress on determining "essential" Islam, is also symptomatic of a tendency within Indian judicial history where the courts interpret what is in essence a Constitutional question—in this case the right of Muslim women students to profess their religion—through a supposed analysis of the religious premises of the petitioners' demand. In denying the students the right to wear the hijab to school, or pre-university, the court's judgement did not restrict itself to the petition that asserted the students' right to religion as enshrined under Article 25 but instead chose to deliberate on whether their idea of the hijab as part of an interpretation of religious practice was permissible under the law. Based on a hair-splitting distinction between 'freedom of conscience' and 'religious expression,' the court maintained that the hijab was merely an outward expression, and not an 'essential religious practice' in Islam.[2] Furthermore, the judges decreed that the uniform promoted the 'principles of secularism,' but also went on to argue that as 'discipline and decorum' were prerequisites of public spaces such as schools, 'reasonable restrictions' could be applied to all other freedoms, such as what one chose to wear. In such a reading, the hijab is both non-secular as it is indisciplined and indecorous!

---

1. Article 25 of the Indian Constitution ensures every citizen four types of religious freedoms—1) freedom of conscience 2) right to profess 3) right to practice 4) right to propagate religion.

2. See https://www.scobserver.in/reports/hijab-ban-judgment-summary-karnataka-hc/

This becomes particularly relevant when historically there is the entire domain of "purdah nasheen" or veiled Hindu women across caste from north India, to Nambudiri Brahmin women in Kerala, whose strict veiling was enforced in order to maintain bodily purity. Such forms of sartorial, or other kinds, of veiling were symbolic of their modesty and decorousness. Consequently, the seclusion that they were expected to follow was designed to achieve such a goal. For large numbers of Hindu communities in north and eastern India that practice purdah (which can range from women covering just their heads with the end of their sari or dupatta[3], to covering their faces) the practice is both a marker of marital kinship, as well as one that represents gendered spatial differentiation. Brides and married women are the ones who usually observe purdah in the presence of their marital male kin, or when leaving their homes—signifying their containment within protected "private" spaces even while venturing out into the public. In the instances where urban Hindu families may have abandoned an older practice of purdah, girls and women who wear salwar kameez, the long tunic and trouser, continue to drape the dupatta over their chest as a mark of their modesty. This is true of the sari too, worn by women all over India, which is wrapped around the entire body and barring the head, face or feet covers every other part of the woman's body.

These examples aside, Indian history is replete with biographical and regional details regarding spatial and sartorial separation of women from men. The seclusion of Nambudiri Brahmin women until well into the post

---

3. Cotton scarf or shawl worn by women across their chests, over their tunics, as a sign of their modesty.

independence period was the outcome of both strict rules regarding caste and sexual purity, and formulated specifically in order to regulate their chastity. The terms used to refer to Nambudiri Brahmin women were antarjanam or akatamma, both of which meant people meant to stay "inside" or in the inner sphere. In fact, these women were never permitted outside on their own, and should they have done so, they were meant to cover their faces with an umbrella [marakuda] and were at all times to be accompanied by a woman servant or companion.[4] In other words, large numbers of Hindu communities have also continually identified sartorial modesty for women as essential for the sustenance of their "culture." The court's assessment that the hijab violated the principle of "decorum" and "discipline" in schools then, is surprising given that Indians across communities define culture and decorum in similar ways.

Striking in the ongoing controversy are the voices of young Muslim women, with or without the hijab, who have been protesting on streets, giving interviews and writing in the press. For the most part I have found, in interviews with the affected students, or statements they have made, that they are clear headed, articulate, and angry about not being allowed to attend class on grounds of a trumped-up excuse. They understand both the politics behind this move as much as they wish to return to their classes. What is striking is that they aren't obsessed, as are their Hindutva detractors on the streets or online, about the hijab. It is a part of them, and gives them a sense of self. And that is all there is to it. Listening to the passionate

---

4. Yalman, Nur. 'On the Purity of Women in the Castes of Ceylon and Malabar.' *The Journal of the Royal Institute of Great Britain and Ireland*, vol. 3, no. 1, 1963, pp. 25-58.

young Muslim women students who have been protesting for their right to wear the hijab has been both moving and enlightening, and I was reminded of Afsaneh Najmabadi's brilliant essay on veiling, where she reads early 20th century male reformist writing in Iran against late 19th century women's critique of patriarchy.[5] In brief, she reads Iran's cultural shifts to argue that while male reformers unveiled women with the objective of rendering them "modern," such "modernized" women could never match the razor sharp, raunchy, rebellious and biting, feminist tongue of their burqa clad forbears.

In other words, the modern Iranian women though unveiled and schooled in new ways were condemned to carry the civilizational burden of a "veiled," as in polite and ultimately docile, tongue. Cutting to the 21st century, it is evident that while there may be some convergence between Islamist ideas of pious subjectivity and those espoused by a generation of younger believers, it is also evident that their sense of self assurance comes not only from Islamist, or are even da'wah inspired, notions of devotion but also from strong strands of criticality (like ijtihad) that are intrinsic to Islamic philosophy. That aside, the ongoing oppositional movements in India, with their repeated references to the Constitution have provided these young women with a language to articulate their rights. Far from being a silent and oppressed lot, they are bright, eloquent and perfectly aware of what they want. Their self confidence and clarity are ample proof of the fact that the hijab has been no hindrance to their education until now.

The history of the veil has shown that both unveiling and

5. Najmabadi, Afsaneh. 'Veiled Discourse–Unveiled Bodies.' *Feminist Studies*, vol. 19, no. 3, Autumn 1993, pp. 487-518.

veiling are complex signifiers that have changing meanings. In India, we have instances of both unveiling and veiling that have been initiated by Indian Muslim women. The early 20th century saw many Muslim women joining the national movement, giving up veiling, feeling this was the only way for them to change their own, and the country's, future. More recently, and in an atmosphere of heightened Islamophobia in India and the world (especially post the demolition of the Babri masjid, followed by 9/11, and the Gujarat carnage), Muslim women in India, like their counterparts across the world, have donned the hijab, naqab and in many instances the burqa. The reasons are varied but at the heart of this is a coming together of a desire for community identity, cultural and political visibility and assertion, and a need to be safe within their own community in bigoted and Islamophobic contexts. In other words, in many instances, the young women wearing the hijab have chosen to do so on their own volition. Having said that, Muslim women's assertion doesn't come only through donning the hijab. As with women of every caste and community there is obviously immense internal difference, be it of political affiliation, forms of articulation, or about ideas of self assertion. Under normal circumstances there would have been no need to state this rather obvious fact. However, in today's India, this needs to be emphasized. The reason for doing so is that while the coming together of Islamophobic and liberal feminist discourses in the West produced the idea (and image) of the oppressed and servile Muslim woman who needs saving (a point Leila Abu-Lughod's superb book *Do Muslim Women Need Saving*[6]

---

6. Abu-Lughod, Lila. *Do Muslim Women Need Saving?* Harvard UP, 2013.

makes very effectively), in Hindutva-ized India, the impulses differ.

While the 'saving Muslim women' [from Muslim patriarchy] impulse can be seen in action in instances like the present government leaping to outlaw the almost dysfunctional practice of "triple talaq,"[7] in India this savior complex is twinned with a far more powerful urge to marginalize Muslims, and subdue them into submission through the use of different forms of violence. In other words, the demand to unveil hijab-clad students in the language of conforming to specific institutional dress codes is designed mainly to humiliate them into submitting to the will of the majority. The "uniform" rather than the hijab is what we must focus our attention on—both as a repressive dress code, and the far more dangerous potential that "uniformity" has for eroding personal laws, and cultural and religious differences within the country.

This is the manner in which the idea of "uniformity" is invoked in the ongoing discussions by the present government on the Uniform Civil Code [henceforth UCC]. As is known to many, the UCC came out of the women's movements' desire, via Ambedkar, to create a non-denominational set of laws that could have the potential for creating greater gender justice, especially in matters considered "personal," i.e. pertaining to marriage, family and inheritance practices. In India at present these matters are governed by religion specific "personal laws." However, by the late 1980s, seeing the potential for its grave misuse in the wake of growing communal violence, women's groups and organizations abandoned the campaign for a UCC that they had pressed

---

7. See https://www.business-standard.com/article/current-affairs/supreme-court-sets-aside-instant-triple-talaq-in-split-verdict-117082300059_1.html

for earlier. Instead, they drafted a variety of options that could be pursued, including the creation of an egalitarian civil code that could be opted for by anyone who wished to do so, irrespective of their birth religion.[8]

Predictably, under the pretext of 'saving Muslim women' the BJP appropriated the demand for a UCC, and this remains the party's purported reason for their now popularized 'one nation, one code' demand. While their desire to "save" Muslim women from polygamy is the argument that is heard most often, it is evident that uniformity, as in homogenizing a country with immense cultural and religious diversity, is what underwrites the Hindutva agenda.[9] The BJP's campaign, based on extreme generalizations, absence of historical detail and context, and immense contradictions between the proclaimed aim and the history of practice is advantageous to them because now the UCC can be presented as a law for the common good that is being opposed by woolly-headed liberals and secularists. A few details about the history of the UCC, its jettisoning, and subsequent retrieval are worth mentioning here.

To begin with, the attempts by BR Ambedkar, Law Minister and one of the chief architects of the Indian Constitution, to render operational both a uniform civil code, and reforms within Hindu law were both jeopardized because of the opposition from both members of the Hindu

8. Rajan, Rajeswari Sundar. 'Women between Community and State: Some Implications of the Uniform Civil Code Debates in India.' *Social Text 65*, vol.18, no. 4, 2000, pp. 55-82.

9. See https://swarajyamag.com/politics/uniform-civil-code-why-bjps-promise-to-enact-a-single-family-law-for-uttarakhand-is-a-significant-development; https://www.indiatoday.in/india/story/uniform-civil-code-benefit-muslim-women-assam-cm-himanta-biswa-sarma-1944183-2022-05-01

Mahasabha and Congress in the 1940s and '50s. The reason was that the patriarchs of the Hindu Right did not wish for any reform of family laws or equal inheritance by daughters and sons to the family property. Though different aspects of Hindu law have now been reformed, the goal of perfect gender equality is still incomplete. Similarly, while the charge against Islam is that it permits polygamy— something that is not statistically supported[10]—the fact that the practice exists amongst Hindus, Buddhists and tribal communities is never addressed. More recently, legal scholar and expert, Professor Faizan Mustafa, demonstrated how the much-admired Goan law permitted Hindu men to marry a second time if their first wives did not give birth to a son by the time they were 30 years of age.[11] In fact, legal scholars like him, Flavia Agnes, and others have argued conclusively that while gender justice, and an equality of rights, is essential, this will not be achieved by legalizing a uniform code. As they suggest, the way forward would be for reform within specific religious personal laws, rather than imposing a UCC that will neither resolve the issues that are at stake, nor translate into everyday practice, as is clear from the many social laws, like dowry prohibition or child marriage abolition, that haven't managed to radically transform existing social practices.[12]

Unless a draft bill is made available for public discussion, it is unclear what is envisaged at present by the BJP when it

---

10. See https://www.counterview.net/2016/09/polygamy-in-india-down-in-45-yrs.html

11. Mustafa, Faizan. 'Are we ready for the Uniform Civil Code?' July 11, 2021. https://www.youtube.com/watch?v=2bvFtH0AItg, July 11, 2021.

12. See https://theswaddle.com/we-asked-six-experts-to-explain-the-impact-of-a-uniform-civil-code-in-modern-india/

speaks of the UCC; in its absence it merely adds to the fear amongst minorities, lawyers and women's groups arguing for gender justice that this is simply a ploy to deprive religious minorities of their right to religious freedom. While the BJP ministers and supporters frequently mention Article 44 of the Indian Constitution[13], it is worth remembering that this is a part of the Directive Principles of the Constitution; in other words, these are guidelines for future action that, as in the case of the UCC, would require consent of communities before it can be promulgated as a law. In this regard, an argument made frequently by social justice activists and feminists that uniformity is not equality, and equality does not mean justice, needs to be reiterated. In a country with a long history of inequality and injustice, not to mention a deeply skewed and asymmetric access to constitutional and other legal provisions[14], the use of the term "uniform" can mean nothing other than an attempt to homogenize the population. Given that the focus of this reform drive has been on minority populations, especially Muslims, it may not be incorrect to assume that the direction of the homogenization drive, via the proposed UCC, will be to make Sharia law and its administrative reach redundant.

It is clear that the BJP has suddenly woken up to the repressive potential of the school uniform, and has decided to transform this opportunity to their advantage. In other

---

13. Article 44 is part of the Directive Principles of the Indian Constitution that says that the 'state shall endeavor to secure a Uniform Civil Code for the citizens throughout the territory of India.' These cannot be enforced by any court, but relevant for governance. https://indianexpress.com/ article/explained/explained-after-cji-bobdes-remarks-on-uniform-civil-code-a-look-at-its-status-debate-around-it-7249410/

14. For one of the best discussions of this, see Jayal, Niraja Gopal. *Citizenship and its Discontents: An Indian History*, Harvard UP, 2013.

words, it is not possible to interpret the saffron party's support for the school uniform, and the attack on the hijab, as isolated or delinked from the larger workings of the Sangh's political agenda. On the contrary, this is in keeping with many recent attempts at erasing the history of Islam from the country—from deleting sections and chapters from school text books to changing names of streets, railway stations and towns with Muslim associations—in many parts of the country. The hijab ban is part of this kind of "cleansing"—in this instance of removing any visual reference to the presence of Islam in the country. That aside, such a move also pushes Muslim students and teachers into a corner, where the options before them become to either comply with the ban by submitting to sartorial homogenization, or to opt out of the mainstream education system. This is particularly dangerous at a time when attacks on the madrasa system are on the increase.[15] We have a Constitution that guarantees Indian citizens a wide variety of rights, including the rights to religion and education. Disallowing hijab-clad students from attending classes, or sitting examinations, is a direct contravention of these rights. Not resisting now will be the triumph of majoritarian bigotry, and its attempts at creating pliant, and infinitely replicable, subjects in a "uniform" nation.

---

15. See https://theprint.in/opinion/indian-madrasas-are-thought-influencers-their-funding-modernisation-should-be-priority/632654/

PART THREE

ETHNO/HISTORY/LIFE WRITING

SUBJUGATION OR SUBJECTIVE LIBERATION

How Purdah Enabled Muslim Women's Social Engagement

Shilujas M.

The word to word meaning of purdah means a curtain or veil, and functionally it refers to the various modes of shielding women from the gaze, primarily of men other than their husbands or men of their natal family, in the South Asian subcontinent. Both the top to toe covering of the entire body or the veiling of parts of the head and face is termed purdah and it also refers to the practice of the seclusion of women inside their homes. Referring to the garb, purdah denotes the praxis of completely covering a woman's body by wearing a loose, body-covering robe called the burqa.

Purdah or the veiling and seclusion of women is a distinct interesting aspect of Indian family life. In several parts of northern and central India, particularly in rural areas, Hindu and Muslim women follow complex rules of veiling their bodies and avoidance of public appearance, especially in the presence of relatives by marriage and strangers. The practice of purdah is inextricably linked to patterns of authority and harmony within the family. Rules of Hindu and Muslim customs of purdah differ in certain key ways, but female modesty and decorum as well as the concepts of family honour are ubiquitous in various forms of purdah. For the women from families that hold higher status, the purdah restrictions are much more rigid than the others.

As in the sense of seclusion and the segregation of men and women, the argument of purdah coming to the Indian subcontinent with Muslim conquests of north India around 1200 CE is of limited historical validity. In popular usage, hijab is defined as the 'headcover and modest dress for women' among Muslims, which most Islamic legal systems define as covering everything except face and hands in public. According to Islamic scholarship, the hijab is ascribed with a wider meaning of modesty, privacy, and morality. The word for a headscarf or veil used in the Quran is Khimar and not hijab. A metaphysical definition of hijab refers to the veil which separates man or the world from God. Since the 1970s, the hijab has emerged as a symbol of Islamic consciousness (Ahmed 1992).

The Quran does not use the term hijab or veil to refer to an article of clothing for women or men, rather it refers to a spatial curtain that divides or provides privacy. The Quran instructed Muslim male believers to talk to the wives of Prophet Muhammad from behind a hijab. This hijab was the responsibility of the men and not the wives of Muhammad. However, this instruction that was specific to the wives of Muhammad, was generalized in later Muslim societies, leading to veiled segregation of Muslim men and women in public. The modesty in Quran concerns garments, gait, the gaze of the genders, and genitalia irrespective of gender (Ahmed 1992: 583).

Muslims in Malabar and Subjective Experience of Purdah

Wearing purdah (a long coat) has become a common practice among Muslims in Kerala, especially during the last two decades and its adoption continues to grow. According to media reports, the number of Muslim women who wear purdah in the five northern districts of the Malabar region with a prominently Muslim population witnessed an increase of 3.5 percent in 1990 to 32.5 in 2005 (Basheer 2001).

Purdah has become more of a cultural feature rather than a religious requirement now. Either way, the system of purdah remains an integral part of everyday life for a large section of people and is a mark of their culture. It is important that women do not passively accept the obligation to purdah, but actively internalize this practice by attributing personal meanings to it. In socio-political discourse, the question of identity and identification are linked to subjectivity and it will become invalid without linking them with the question of subjectivity.

In an anthropological study of the phenomenon of new veiling in the context of Kerala, Mathhea Agnes (2004), who was a student of Amsterdam University, analyzes the practice of purdah in Kerala society and tried to seek answers to the question as to whether women contribute to their own submissive position. He examines how local, national and global agencies influence the decision of young and educated Muslim women to dress differently and how it affects their engagement in the public sphere.

First, he explains how the rise in purdah observance

is connected with a new ideal religiosity, shaped through politics, education and increasing contact with the Gulf. Examining the changing role of women in Kerala society, Agnes argues that the recent emphasis on purdah reveals the fundamental changes in social and hierarchical relationships due to these modern developments. Agnes pointed out that to understand how women act as agents, one must pay attention to the limitations they face as well as the possibilities they have. Shedding light on the significance of family and community in the decision of the individual woman, he raises doubts about the autonomy of agency. The meaning-giving capacity reveals that the acceptance to dress in a certain way is by no means a passive process but instead must be seen as an act of agency (Agnes 2004: 1-5).

Agnes (2004) concludes that dressing is never a neutral practice determined by taste or fashion, rather it is a means to manage and express identities. This is done both by the women themselves as by other social forms of authorities that assert control over the female body. The dress style of individual women reproduces social and normative values but also expresses individual ideas and desires and must therefore be regarded as a social act. Subsequently, changes in dress style indicate changes in existing cultural ideas and shifts in social and hierarchical relationships.

Agnes sees that purdah observance in Kerala does not reflect traditionalism, but typifies the ideal modern Muslim woman instead. Many things discussed—gender relationships, safety and danger, social control and reputation, individuality and adjustment—are not confined to the Muslim community, but are important for other Malayalee women as well (Agnes 2004: 96-97).

Much of these discussions on purdah revolve around the question of interpretation of the religio-social setting in which such practices gain meanings. The studied Muslim community in Malabar is far from monolithic, although purdah is pivotal in identity formation. For instance, for some women, the veil is indeed an indispensable practice and a means for both one's being and becoming religious. While some are self-conscious about the impact of their dress style, others never really questioned whether or not it was important to veil. And even while some are enabled by purdah, others accept this dress for relating themselves with the community, family and others.

Even if purdah wearing can be a part of patriarchal impositions, there are instances where it becomes preferable for the one who wears it. That is, just like power is enabling, purdah is also enabling; this may not be the case always, but at the same time there are such events and fluid preferences. There is no denial that purdah does have oppressive and suppressive attributes, which has already been pointed out by several researchers. The practice of purdah assumes a different meaning when individuals choose a certain dress code to relate with others as well as with oneself through dressing up one's body, and thus somebody is benefiting in purdah. There are several moments of preference as wearing purdah appears to oneself as one's own choice. The theoretical assumption is that no individual is monolithic and has multiple selves. In other words, one's choice need not be because of one reason but multiple reasons and considerations that are her own. At least that is one of the responses that can be termed as experiential.

For Others, but for Me Too

Sabeena, a 39-year-old woman and a dependent of a Gulf migrant husband, started to wear purdah at the age of 34.

There was an "other" who persuaded her to do so. During the telephonic conversations between the wife and husband, he suggested that as 'our children are growing old, it is better you begin to wear purdah.' This is a moment when there is a need to shift one's dressing habit to accommodate another situation. This is not so much an acceptance of a shift in dress code that one has to follow, but a shift in the habit of dressing oneself for oneself. She had been habituated to wearing saris since adulthood, but she could not respond to her husband's suggestion negatively. Then she "opted"—the question of self-will is not considered here—to wear purdah whenever she goes out of the home. Now she begins to shift her presentation of self to others through purdah. At the beginning with mild remorse, but later, she said: 'I began to find it is fine for different reasons.'

Here, we find that the beginning of a shift in the followed dressing pattern could be due to persuasion from others, but over time, it becomes self-persuasive to the recipient of persuasion. Here, by persuasion we do not mean seduction, for such a shift only enabled her to refashion herself for herself; the cause of this acceptance to shift one's dressing style does not matter in every life. Rather, she found functional use due to such a shift in her dress. Perhaps, the origin of persuasion might have appeared to them as an irrelevant factor in the acceptance, except at the moment of the beginning of making a new dress to be worn over their bodies. In short, one begins to dress one's body in terms of others' eye-point, without much friction.

Self-Identification in Congregation

Self-identification as a concept resonates with another concept of intersubjectivity. When an individual is among others, he/she will be positioned to think of oneself in relation to others who were congregated and with whom that individual strived to identify. Such congregations take place on the occasions of marriage, Quran teaching, death etc. In this sub-category, there are two discernible types. The first one is wearing purdah to identify oneself with others of the congregation. The other is, occasions in which sari is preferred by otherwise purdah-wearing women, such as at marriage congregations. This typology suggests that there is no single dress code of a community as a whole but there are only different ways of being with others clad in one or another robe.

Twenty-six-year-old Hajara wears a sari or salwar kameez when she attends occasions such as weddings or housewarming, that is, within an intimate congregation. She said: 'When everybody wears sari or any other fashionable dresses in wedding functions or so, it is not proper to wear purdah to be with them. Apart from that, such functions are the only chance for poor people like us to show some fashion. I feel at odds in sari if others are in purdah.'

A close reading of Hajara's statement leads to another proposition, however tentative it is, about self-identification. Unlike in the earlier instance, here, there is no persuasion from outside, but a longing to be identified with, it is this longing that influences her choice of dress. One may perhaps probe into her self-preference to know what constituted it. Probably there may be conditions that influenced her "self-preference" are one of the observations that we can make.

Sameera, a 38-year-old woman with two daughters, and belonging to a lower middle-class family, wishes to identify with others of her preferred congregation of Quran class. When she joined the classes, all others were in purdah, except very few, and she was in a sari. Within a short span of time, she began to feel a kind of alienation from her partners in the class. Without any recommendation from outside, she started wearing purdah whenever she attended the classes to avoid isolation. Sameera said: 'I and a few others who were not wearing purdah felt total separation and inferiority among others. The purdah-clads lingered around the meeting place, even after the classes were over, discussing many other matters of common interests. But we left the place immediately after the Quran classes.'

Asmabi, another woman at Mughadar Beach at Kozhikode in northern Kerala, attests to the inferences made above. She said: 'Purdah is a convenience for us to cover our poverty, however, I wear a sari when I go to functions like weddings in the families of our economic status. On several occasions, I had faced insulting comments from people of my own class for wearing purdah. It makes me feel inferior and isolated.' The responses quoted here clearly reveal that there are instances of women who are not adherent to the dress code, altering it according to propriety to be followed in different situations.

Tuning in to Family Norms

A dress that one chooses need not be of one's own choice, but at the same time when one identifies with a profession or any institutions such as family, then also the importance of dress wanes; what predominates is the identification. Since family or house and home are important to existence, identification with either of them or all of them becomes imperative as far as any individual is concerned.

A 47-year-old, upper-class housewife, Kutsiya, was on a morning walk in the jogging track of Sarovaram bio-park in Kozhikode city. She was in purdah. Kutsiya's family migrated to Kozhikode from the Muslim-dominated city of Bhatkal in Karnataka. She was in the habit of wearing purdah right from her childhood as part of their family norm. Kautsiya narrates that Muslim girls in her home village in Bhatkal begin to observe purdah and niqab right from adolescence. 'Purdah is an integral part of our lifestyle. No other form of attire is familiar to me, nor anybody in my family can even think about a dress without purdah,' she said. Notably, even after their migration, they continued the dress code with greater vigour, as even for celebrations like a marriage where more unfamiliar faces gather, she chooses to wear purdah.

Sujatha converted to Islam and changed her name to Sajitha at the age of 25. She was 28-years-old and belonged to a lower-class family residing in the Bangladesh Colony of Kozhikode. She converted to Islam after marrying a Muslim youth. Her mother-in-law and sisters-in-law had been wearing purdah, although she was not following this dress code at the beginning of her married life. When she experienced isolation in her husband's family, she thought of switching to purdah. Sajitha said: 'I had no option of returning to my home because I married a man outside my caste. My sisters-in-law were hesitant to take me along with them to any function outside the colony. Two years back I started to wear purdah like them and thus became more acceptable to them, and now I feel that I have become one among them.' The self-identification with family and to be one among the members of that family is explicit and emphasized here. That means identification of Sajitha as part of "we" by others and her self-identification with them is anchored on the dressing.

Doctrinal Identification

As purdah is a dress that is worn exclusively by Muslim women, therefore, it has to be stubbornly connected to religious codes and norms. The religious institutions need not impose it directly, but the dress code followed by a community "naturally" gets transmitted to succeeding generations. For instance, the headgear of the Sikhs gets transmitted to their sons more or less automatically. In such instances, what one wears is never considered to be a matter of self-choice or the free will of individuals.

Habeeba belongs to a middle-class family of Thalassery in the Kannur district of northern Kerala. According to her, the only attraction with purdah was that it upholds the religious strictures on female dress code as it does not expose the body. She said that during her adolescence, purdah was not in vogue and the significations of purdah were not much discussed in the family. She stated, 'it was purely my decision to wear purdah when it was getting popular throughout Kerala. Being a Muslim woman, wearing a hijab gives me a sense of protection when I am in public. I feel that in this clothing my body shape would not become a topic of discussion for men at large.'

Sakkeena began wearing purdah about ten years ago and she is 47 years old now and belongs to a middle-class family in Kozhikode. Sakkeena says she became aware of the need for a religious dress code after she became an activist of a religious organization called Ittihadul Syubbanul Mujahideen (ISM). The Quran classes attended by new women activists like Sakkeena were emphatic about religious stipulations for women to conceal their whole body except their hands and face. Sakeena said, 'during the organizational meetings at the masjids, when women are allowed to take part in prayer, most of the women were in purdah. It encouraged me to switch to purdah. It was my natural and spontaneous choice. No element of pressure was there on my decision.' The religious congregation and unsaid transmission of a dress code are evident here. When a majority of one's peer group follow a dress code then one is tempted to mimic the majority as it is in any religious or cultural observations of norm-bound behaviour.

Covering the Body

Though religious dictums insist that women cover their bodies when they are in public places before strangers, there could be non-religious dimensions, too, such as to avoid any suspicion about the body. That is, since religion stipulates to cover the body with purdah if a woman has a complex that some parts of her body may appear ugly or is disgusting to others, then purdah can come to aid as it covers the entire body. Here, rather than covering the whole body, covering the parts which one likes to hide attains a more important function of purdah wearing.

Purdah covers both beauty and the burns of life. Perhaps Rasiya's expressions and presentation of self elucidate this rather metaphorical statement. Rasiya was 35 years of age and a resident of the Bangladesh colony in Kozhikode. She said, 'my body was burnt from neck to belly and its scars are all over my torso. When discharged from hospital, I realized that the scars and wounds of burns have made my body horrible to be seen.' It was at this point of time, she decided to wear a purdah to cover up her burn marks. More than anything else, what we find here is the enabling or functional quality of purdah wearing. That is, as much as displaying the body, covering it also may become part of life.

Forty-seven-year-old Khadeeja was a member of a working-class fishing dwelling at the Nainamvalappu Beach in Kozhikode. She had been wearing purdah for five years. She thinks that she is fat and dark-complexioned and therefore unattractive. She was humiliated at public functions. Khadeeja accepted purdah to hide her "uncharming" body. Khadeeja said, 'Now I don't care about the darkness of my skin. After I started wearing purdah people stare less at me. Even if I don't have good ornaments, I can travel with confidence in purdah without any worry of others noticing it.' Here, what is more glaring is that certain lacks and perceived deformities of one's body can be buried under the purdah and thus enable social engagement.

Covering of the Colourful or Colourless

Suharabi is 39-years-old and lives with her three children in Marad Beach on the outskirts of Kozhikode. They are lower-class day labourers. Suharabi says it was her own choice to wear purdah. She said, 'I was attracted to purdah when I saw others in it. It was my own decision to wear purdah. Since our family is financially poor, we did not have enough ornaments to wear. When we went out in sari, we used to borrow gold or other ornaments from the neighbours, which was embarrassing for me. When purdah became a habit, ornaments became irrelevant. If we are wearing purdah with a muftha, not even an earring is needed.' Once again, her preference for purdah is out of a sense of lack and the purdah here covers her material deprivation as symbolized by gold and not her body.

Thirty-four-year-old Aminabi, belonging to a lower-class family, pointed out another context. When her family buys clothes for them on Eid, money will not be sufficient to purchase for the whole family, but only for the children. To conceal the fact the mother has no money to purchase new clothes for herself she chose purdah. No one would ask about the new dress and no one bothers about whether the purdah is old or new. Or at least such questions are preempted. Certifying the same, 30-years-old Asmabi said, 'It is not possible for us to buy costly sarees and matching blouses. Ornaments are clearly out of our financial status. So purdah is convenient to me to cover my poverty.'

The Veil and Morality

Purdah comes in between family members of an extended family or even a nuclear family to uphold the moral codes that they collectively share. It is worth mentioning that there is no interstice between moral codes and dress codes even when intimate kinship bound individuals interact. Purdah enables, in this sense, retention of one's desired moral code. There are instances in which the desire for the retention of the moral code emanates from both men and women.

Asiya, who was with her ailing daughter in Kozhikode Beach Hospital, is 47-years-old and belongs to a middle-class family. Asiya started wearing purdah eight years ago as a result of repeated inadvertent expressions of her sons-in-law's wish that she should wear a purdah. Asiya said, 'My sons-in-law didn't directly tell their wish to see their mother-in-law in a purdah, but they communicated through my daughters and when one of the sons-in-law came with purdah as a gift, I had no option but to wear it to avoid his displeasure.'

What has to be pointed out here is that the desire of the sons-in-law for their mother-in-law to wear purdah comes from self-preventing any chance or non-moral or non-religious relation with her. In their community, the age gap between mother-in-law and their sons-in-law is sexually seductive. Perhaps that is why Asiya had to start wearing purdah. If, in this case, the source initiation was men, there are other examples in which women are the source of persuasion.

Sulaikha was on a leisure trip in Sarovaram Bio-park, an amusement avenue in Kozhikode, accompanied by her two daughters and their husbands. At forty Sulaikha lives at Koduvally in Kozhikode. She said, 'There was tremendous pressure from my daughters to change myself into purdah. Both of my daughters suggested that it would be better if I wear purdah when I go to public gatherings. One daughter even asked her husband to bring a purdah for me from the Gulf.' Here, the feeling of a possible breach of moral code comes from her daughters. That means, in retaining the moral code of families there is not much difference, be it a man or woman, purdah comes as a saviour. Here purdah is preferred because it is the saviour to satisfy their desire to retain the moral codes related to sexuality. These two instances primarily show the blurred distinction between the genders, at least in this specific or micro-specific instance of the culture of wearing purdah. Of course, the central observation is that purdah comes into moral, sexual and kinship codes within the family structure, even in the mutual relations among the family members.

Obligations

Here the decision is driven by obligations that one bears to a code of behavioural patterns. These obligations can be to God, family, some or other individual or institution etc. Obligations sometimes result in altering one's habituated or customary behaviour. Here obligations need not be considered as power from above or obligation that is imposed.

Fifty-year-old Sameena of an upper-class family of Kozhikode had this to say: 'Earlier I used to wear fashionable dresses. But after attending some Quran classes, I realized that my dressing is un-Islamic. Religious talks and Quran classes emphasized the need for Islamic dressing to conceal the *aurah* of women. I became afraid of God's punishment for unlawful dressing. The Quran classes repeatedly reminded of the punishment of God towards morally loose women, who wear fashionable dresses.' In this instance, one could mark the obligation to God as the directive principle for Sameena to wear purdah. No doubt fear of punishment also fuelled her thoughts. The initiation here is the obligation to God and the fear of punishment that work as the initiating factors.

Functionality and material repeatability of purdah wearing was the omnipresent aspect in all the instances discussed here. It is one's own rationality that led the individuals to wear purdah. Of course, the rationalities and contexts change considerably as we have already seen. The positive, permissive and enabling dimensions of purdah can be exemplified with insights from these instances.

Women without Purdah and the Male Gaze

Women get their exclusive space without the gaze on several occasions, the most important and frequent one being marriage ceremonies. Weddings in rich Muslim families are worth seeing for their luxuriance and extravaganza. Men and women gather separately for the function and the marriage feast is held separately too. Women, who otherwise wear purdah, are not at all reluctant to wear a sari and other fashionable outfits. They are comfortable in the women-only gathering. It will be revealing to address the question of how women, who usually wear purdah, feel free without it. Here, the removal of purdah or being without it is to do more with sociality and gender proximity.

Kutsiya said, 'I wear purdah even when I attend social functions in Kozhikode, but at my home place, I need not wear it during the marriage functions because no men other than close blood relatives are allowed into the area where only we women sit.'

Ameena, aged 30, with an economically upper-class family background and residing in Kozhikode, made it clear that when she goes to festive occasions in purdah, she would switch to sari or salwar kameez once she reaches the venue. She said, 'When we are travelling by bus or train the public will see us in fashionable dresses. But at the wedding functions, only the blood relatives are gathered and we need not bother about our dressing.' On such occasions, purdah will not be worn and would be in the bag or in the shelves of the neighbouring house.

Forty-five-year-old Fathima, who is a member of a rich religious family at Madai[1] in Kannur, says that she used to wear a sari while attending family functions. But after she turned 40, Fathima started using purdah regularly.

Sabeena, aged 39, believes that sari or salwar kameez can be used at functions in Kozhikode, where she stays, because there is no chance for mingling with men as feasts and gatherings in connection with weddings etc. are held

---

1. Madai is one of the rare Muslim populated area of Kerala, where the *purdah*-clad women lead the family since their male members are mostly in the gulf.

separately for men and women. 19-year-old Shaana, who comes from the affluent Barami[2] family at Kuttichira in Kozhikode, is a student of BBA in the prestigious Providence Women's College. She said purdah protects her from ugly staring on her body. She interestingly commented: 'There are several male teachers, though the college is girls-only. The fellow students are non-Muslims in the majority. We are allowed to give up the religious dress code only before blood relatives. In all other circumstances, a sort of segregation is preferred. I don't use purdah on festive occasions or family get-togethers. For such functions, I choose salwar kameez with full sleeves and a headscarf to cover my head. But one disadvantage of salwar kameez compared to purdah is that it cannot be used for namaz because then, additional socks should be used.'

It is not that women cannot be present at all in the public arena without purdah, but there are occasions where they go without it and purdah wearing women in Malabar make the most of such occasions. Here also, purdah does not come as an impediment to one's freedom, but as something disposable, there are possibilities of being in their community without it.

Display of the Displayable

There are occasions for women to present themselves among others without purdah. The question of displayability comes into the picture mainly because purdah is a cover and covering of the body is normal, but at the same time, presentation of oneself in celebrations without purdah is a celebration of non-normal occasions. Presentation of self in

---

2. Barami is a wealthy business clan of Muslim community migrated from outside Kerala.

the realm of public visibility becomes something desirable. Several women expressed their interest in attending festivals, weddings etc where they get a legitimate occasion to wear sari or churidar and ornaments. On such occasions, women prefer not to cover themselves in purdah and choose the occasion to display their pomp and prosperity. I found that this behaviour was more pronounced among middle-class women.

Sakkeeena, a 47-year-old woman of a middle-class family, says that women like her get rare chances to show off their ornaments, such as only in wedding functions. Sakkeena said: 'I prefer sari for family functions like weddings, but it is because others also prefer that during festive occasions.'

These moments and instances enable the women to engage in public without their purdah and assists the display of one's both natural and acquired endowments.

Major Observations

Purdah is not just a custom of "covering-up" of the female body. Women consider it more as a "dress" for their body and thus they fashion themselves in purdah to be congruent with a community or occasion. Purdah makes a woman available to see herself. Contrary to the popular notion that purdah secludes and subjugates, a lot of women experience it in another way. While women from the lower classes find purdah helpful to conceal many of their insufficiencies by making it their default dress, a few others find it as a comfortable outfit within which they can hide their physical disabilities. For many women, a rather "offensive" purdah helps them fit in during an occasion or in a community as wearing it makes them more acceptable and strengthens them to overcome the sense of alienation and guilt.

Covering themselves with purdah liberates women from the image of being an object of sex. Within purdah, a woman doesn't have to bother about her body or appearance. To most, within purdah she can leave her worries about others' interrogating stares into her probity or fashion. Purdah helps a woman get freedom from others, because she doesn't have to bother about what she wears inside the purdah.

The other conveniences shared by the "purdah-wearing women" were that these outfits made them feel secure, and provided self-confidence in their daily life. Another point is that purdah helped to save money, as women need not spend lavishly on costly apparel and ornaments; lack or absence of ornaments gets covered by purdah and no one bothers about what is beneath the purdah.

In many cases, mothers-in-law receive purdah as a gift from their sons-in-law. In fact, the daughters want their mothers to wear purdah and they convince the mothers that their husbands wish their in-laws to do so. This, maybe, is because the daughters develop a 'fear of incest' (Barnhart 1992: 20) within their subconscious.

Most of the women believe that purdah is an Islamic dress code and consider it as the most suitable attire for Muslim women. It was also clear that most of the "purdah-wearing women" prefer to wear sarees and churidars on special occasions like wedding ceremonies, family gatherings etc. The justifications for preferring sarees or churidars on such occasions also vary as per the class the women belong to. Upper-class women justified it that according to the Quran, there is no need to wear purdah before other Muslim women and the men who are close blood relatives.

The basic notions behind wearing purdah varies according to class, notions about modesty and aristocracy persuaded upper-class women to prefer purdah in general.

But the middle-class women prefer purdah mainly as part of the process of identification. Primarily these women want to identify themselves with others during an occasion or to a community in which they belong. So they prefer to wear purdah to identify with the other women around them who are already wearing purdah. Purdah enables poor women to hide their economic and physical insufficiencies or disabilities.

Conclusions

The dress becomes a code in the identification and presentation of self-identity and the relation between dress and self-identification coincides. For instance, it is not difficult to distinguish a Buddhist monk or a Christian nun from others, just because of their appearance in a particular dress that is coded. Religion is ingrained in one's dress; even if one is a trans-dress code person, even then, it works as a code to identify that transgression. The dressing is placed within several symbolic relations. About self-identification, more than identification, it is entrenched in relations of signification, functionality and relations of power. This is because self-identification involves not only relations with others but also relations with oneself. Clothing one's body or leaving it bare can be seen as a way of dressing; that is, presenting one's body. Dress as a code of self-identification was inextricably linked to identification as well, whenever they have intersected and questions of selfhood came to prominence; in other words, the central questions were anchored on the concept of "subjectivity." The word "cover" got metaphorically reduced to a particular dress belonging to a particular religion with gender specificity.

Purdah is no more a dress alone, but an ornament, a shield, a protector, a camouflage, a sign and also a free-floating signifier. Purdah prevents and permits; it covers what can be shown and it also covers what is to be hidden. The power of persuasion of wearing purdah is the power ingrained in the identity formations and self-presentations and the acceptance of wearing purdah could be due to coercive force from above or non-coercive force. The significations of wearing purdah are indeterminable. It is probable that one can conceive "purdah-wearing" as effective and affective figures of speech that "covers" even the soul that one beholds as the most desirable.

References

Agnes de Jong, Matthea. *A Moral Dress for Modern Women: Female Muslim Students in Kerala Interpreting the Veil* [Unpublished M.A. Dissertation], University of Amsterdam, 2004.

Ahmed, Leila, *Women and Gender in Islam: Historical Roots of a Modern Debate.* Yale UP, 1992.

Aslam, Reza, *No God But God: The Origin, Evolution, and Future of Islam.* Random House, 2005.

Barnhart, Clarence. L and Robert K. Barnhart. Editors. *The World Book Encyclopedia*, vol. 7 F. Chicago, 1992, p.20

Basheer, M.P. "Malayalam Magazines Drive Women into Purdah." www.thehoot.org/June2001

Desouza, Eunice. *Purdah: An Anthology.* Oxford UP, 2004.

Engineer, Asgar Ali. *The Quran, Women and Modern Society.* Sterling, 1999.

Foucault, Michel. "The Subject and Power." *Michel Foucault: Beyond Structuralism and Hermeneutics.* Edited by Hubert L.Dreyfus and Paul Rabinow. Hemel Hempstead, 1982. pp. 208

___, Michel. *The Use of Pleasure, The History of Sexuality, Vol.2.* Translated by Robert Hurley. Vintage Books 1990.

Jeffrey, Patricia. *Frogs in a Well, Indian Women in Purdah.* Vikas Publishing House 1979.

Moududi, Abul A'la and Maulana Sayyid, *Purdah and the Status of Women in Islam.* Translated by Al-Ash'ari. Markazi Maktaba Islami Pzublishers, 2006.

"The issue of Muslim veiling." *Wikipedia.* http;//en.wikipedia.org/wiki/The issue of Muslim veiling.

UNDERSTANDING SECULARISM
What Shall I Wear to School?

Sweta Dutta

In my short-lived experience as a middle school history teacher, I was introduced to several pedagogical practices and oriented myself with various tools of teaching and knowledge dissemination. This was my first real job where I soon realized that I could no longer dress as a college-goer in shabby clothes. Sometimes through intended and suggestive remarks I was made aware of my immediate setting—middle-aged colleagues who would indulge in long conversations where the central theme was the competitive desire to flaunt expensive sarees, shoes and other personal belongings. The school attracted and catered to the wealthy class across Delhi NCR (National Capital Region). Although I was never made to feel conscious about my appearance by my students, I remember my first nervous interaction with 6th graders.

Middle school students are young adults in transition who require a holy trio of patience, understanding and maturity to work with. I would insist that social science classes were a platform for everyone to share ideas, argue and express oneself fearlessly. Initially it was a challenge to make each student vocalise their thoughts, but I was fortunate enough to witness some terrific transformations—the shy hesitant ones gradually took interest in demonstrating their opinions ever so emphatically in class.

The good old NCERT (National Council of Educational Research and Training) textbook was our stipulated reading. Coming from an ICSE (Indian Certificate of Secondary Education) board, I had read sanitized and grossly assembled fact-based Euro-centric history writing while growing up. The CBSE (Central Board of Secondary Education) social science curriculum on the other hand is structured such that lectures can rarely be didactic in class thus putting emphasis on student-led interactions as the basis to begin any discussion. I remember being incredibly excited about reading and researching on specific topics that I could never imagine having read in school while learning about India's past. Discussions in class ranged from the Delhi Sultan Muhammad-bin-Tughluq's erratic decision to change capitals in medieval sultanate times to the present-day political regime's insistent efforts at rampantly re-naming Mughal/Sultanate/Muslim city, street, stadium, monument after Hindu politicians.

'Why does the government want to call Firoz Shah Kotla stadium as Arun Jaitly stadium?' a charged-up Kirat* enquired. (Arun Jaitly was the former Finance Minister of India, member of the Bharatiya Janata Party.)

'That is because this government is focused on majoritarian politics, wants to appease its voters and saffronize every aspect of Islamic history and culture in India,' answered a fellow seventh grader with conviction.

Even though I was extremely impressed with my students' observations and reasoning, I had to maintain a "diplomatic" stance and let my students answer their own questions when they bordered on political issues. I was warned by the school authorities to never engage in discussions with students in a classroom setting that would incite opinions on electoral politics. Instead, I was instructed to craftily dodge them with responses like "no comments" or dissuade their queries with generic replies like 'you would figure it out eventually.' As a student of history, it was hard for me to practice separating the personal from the political. I would constantly think of innovative ways to critically engage with my students and help them hold up their spirit of questioning. These were adolescents who were able to connect events of the past and questioned their present—what more could I have wanted as a teacher? In dealing with such challenges in everyday interactions with students, I soon found myself being more aware of what to teach rather than being conscious of what I was wearing to school.

At the beginning of this year a dispute pertaining to school uniforms was reported from Udupi, in the Indian State of Karnataka. The row began when some Muslim students who wore Hijab to classes were denied entry on the grounds that it was a violation of the school's strict uniform policies. It soon became a raging political affair when Hindu students backed by the Hindu nationalist organisations like Akhila Bharatiya Vidyarthi Parishad, Vishwa Hindu Parishad and Bajrang Dal, started counter-protests in colleges across Karnataka demanding to wear saffron scarves to classes. The Karnataka High court intervened and issued an order stating that school uniform codes must be strictly followed, ruling hijab as non-essential to Islamic faith. Controversies poured in from all quarters and the civil society reacted adequately to the ban of hijab in educational institutions calling it an attack on fundamental rights. Some others defended the court ruling stating it as a step to maintain "status-quo" in schools and colleges.

A year back while teaching the chapter "Understanding Secularism" to my eighth graders, I was faced with severe challenges to substantiate the need to uphold and express religious identities in the public sphere. The NCERT textbook defines secularism as per the Indian Constitution— the separation of state from religion. The character of Indian secularism is described as follows:

1) That one religious community does not dominate another

2) That some members do not dominate others of the same religious community 3) that the State does not enforce any particular religion nor take away the religious freedom of individuals.

Initially most of the conversation was around discrimination, exclusion and persecution on the grounds of religion—students would cite Junaid Khan's death and other examples of mob lynching from around the country in the last few years. It was important for us to remind ourselves that religious identities necessarily constitute personal choices, and in democratic societies the practice of secularism was the only way to ensure the protection of freedom of individual choices. The confusion however arose while discussing the three ways in which the Indian State practices secularism: a) principled distancing b) non-interference c) intervention.

The first way in which the Indian state prevents the domination of a religious group (the one belonging to the majority) over another is by distancing itself from religion.

This means that 'government spaces like law courts, police stations, government schools and offices are not supposed to display or promote any one religion'. The next effective way the State ensures the absence of religious discrimination is through a strategy of non-interference. This means that 'in order to respect the sentiments of all religions and not interfere with religious practices, the State makes certain exceptions for particular religious communities.' As an example a storyboard described how two friends who have recently bought scooters were meeting for a ride together where one of the friends, a Sikh youth, explained to his friend how the Indian law doesn't require him to wear a helmet while riding a scooter, while his Hindu friend was bound to follow the law failing which he would be subjected to pay a fine.

Now after having read the earlier instance of Indian State distancing itself from religious affairs in government spaces, this might seem like a paradox. What was therefore necessary for us to discuss was how the state cannot force a person to do something that might directly harm, threaten or interfere with one's religious practices and beliefs. The Indian State recognizes that wearing a *pagri* (turban) is 'central to a Sikh's religious practice and in order not to interfere with this, allows an exception in the law.' The final strategy adopted by the Indian State to practice secularism is thus through a strategy of intervention. This essentially means the State can intervene in matters to end social evils like untouchability which is tied to Hindu religious practice since it violates the fundamental rights of a minority population.

Most of the students found it difficult to understand the constant contradictions in these strategies.

'So you are telling me, Ankur* can wear his *pagri* to school but I can't come wearing a saffron dhoti like Baba Ramdev does?' asks a confused Shreyas*.

'The only cool thing about Baba Ramdev is his long hair, not his attire,' added Arjun*.

'Yeah, at least that would make me look like a rockstar!' giggled Rohan*.

The contextual reading and understanding of secularism enabled by the Indian Constitution is not something that is discussed in school teaching. The hijab controversy when contextualized within the State of Karnataka can be viewed from multiple aspects of socio-political churnings. There were disputes on wearing hijab to educational institutions even before 2022, but it did not blow up to an extent where it became a cause for Indian media channels to run prime time national debates on the issue. The reason lies in the rise of Hindutva politics, spearheaded by the Bharatiya Janata Party. But as my student stated his confusion, I am forced to rethink this too—so why does the Indian state adopt so many strategies that constantly contradict each other in order to be a secular state? If the State truly distances itself from religion, and does not take sides, how come it can intervene and make exceptions for some? Why do Muslim women wearing hijabs need rescuing from a secular state that simultaneously rules out a verdict in favour of a right-wing ruling party in the Ayodhya case which practically laid the foundation to build a Hindu Rashtra?

In order to refrain from jumping to a liberal justification of how educational spaces should be sacrosanct, non-political spaces, where the process of knowledge dissemination is muted by religion, culture and language, let us pay careful attention to how constitutional laws and rights are taught in schools. There is a complete naturalization and assumption around the process of understanding secularism from our growing years as children. There hardly lies an effort on the part of the facilitator/educator to celebrate the idea that India is a secular, democratic republic. Not in the sense of chest-thumping pride of belongingness to a nation-state, but truly introspect and understand the nuances of what constitutes the character of a secular state.

We can no longer rely on our "larger" understandings of meanings around constitutional rights and reforms. Young adults being isolated from electoral politics and the understanding of politics is the sign of an educational system and a society which is ready to infantilize a 6th or 7th grader, when in reality their political awareness in today's world of information overload is what shapes the political narrative for tomorrow. In this context, the system must embrace and shape school-going teenagers as political beings who will decide the trajectory of how the nation understands and responds to nuanced ideas like secularism.

In middle and high school humanities classes, the understanding of the Indian constitution can be a stepping stone towards a future for India where hijab bans in educational institutions are not discussed as infotainment across media outlets with a hidden agenda of burying the beauty, nuances and complexities of the Indian constitution. Teachers, specifically social science teachers across the country, should take a lesson from the current controversies to reset and rewind their approaches to impart an understanding of the Indian constitution among the upcoming generation. One might argue that this is asking too much of teachers. Fundamental rights, secular and socialist principles that the larger federal structure of India is constituted of, demands a refined comprehension. Both government and private schools should ideally focus on re-structuring curricula where secular ideals are expounded conceptually and critically aided by sufficient examples from present day social and political narratives. As an instance, eighth graders must learn from the Shah Bano case and the ensuing legislation that the concept of personal laws in religious communities are subject to scrutiny, change and modification by the State law and that is also one of the aspects of Indian secularism, which sets it apart from secular ideas practiced in other democratic nations like America and France. The one significant way in which Indian secularism differs from French/American secularism is how American and French states discourage religious influence in state-politics and follow a strict non-interference policy in religious activities. For instance, in February 2004, France passed a law banning students from wearing religious apparels, such as the Islamic headscarf or the Jewish skullcap or the Sikh turban. Indian secularism on the other hand expounds the idea of positive intervention in religious matters based on the ideals laid out in the Indian Constitution. The 1985 Muhammad Ahmad Khan vs. Shah Bano was a controversial maintenance lawsuit in India, in which the Supreme Court delivered a judgment favouring maintenance given to an aggrieved divorced Muslim woman. Although Shah Bano won the right to alimony from her husband, there was widespread criticism among the Muslim community as to how the court judgement was a direct violation of the Islamic law. Following this, the Congress government introduced the Muslim Women Act, whereby Muslim women could claim alimony from their former husbands till 90 days after the divorce, thus diluting the

Supreme Court's judgement. The Shah Bano case is an excellent example to understand how the Indian state is designed to intervene in religious affairs (here religious/ personal laws) in order to protect the rights of individuals, prevent discrimination and uphold the spirit of secularism in public discourse.

The hijab row for me is a call for attention to policy makers, curriculum designers and educators—we need the school going youth to read, understand, debate and engage with the Indian constitution. It can fulfill the need of the current political regime to instill patriotism among the youth in the way that it was designed to be by the founding fathers of modern independent India and at the same time call for better informed debates, discussions, consultations on issues like the hijab row in the future.

In recent news following the Karnataka high court ruling, seven teachers have been suspended for allowing Muslim students wearing hijab to write their exams. This circles back to freedom entitled to the gatekeepers of the future generation who continue to face the brunt of the law for believing and practicing ideas enshrined in the Indian Constitution. Collectively as a society we need to assess the risk that we are putting both teachers and students in to develop a consciousness on rights and responsibilities that reflect the very soul of the country. A relook at the NCERT Social Science grade eight textbook can help us inculcate a sharper understanding of secularism in an age where voices of protest are continuously stifled, freedom of speech is threatened, and individual choices are questioned and curbed by an ever-vigilant police-state. This can also perhaps be a lesson to put all disputes to an end as muslim women and all those who wish to proudly embrace and understand the meaning of Indian secularism never have to agonise over what to wear to school.

'The Indian State is secular and works in various ways to prevent religious domination. The Indian Constitution guarantees Fundamental Rights that are based on these secular principles. However, this is not to say that there is no violation of these rights in Indian society. Indeed it is precisely because such violations happen frequently that we need a constitutional mechanism to prevent them from happening. The knowledge that such rights exist makes us sensitive to their violations and enables us to take action when these violations take place.'—Chapter 2: 'Understanding Secularism', in *Social and Political Life-III: Textbook for Class VIII.*

---

*All names have been changed to secure the identity of concerned individuals.

IN THE NAME OF HIJAB

Preeti Singh

Clad in a burqa, on the crowded lanes of Charminar, Aleema has a bangle stall. Crowded with food shops, markets, shops, stalls, Charminar has one of the busiest lanes in Hyderabad. Aleema is a mother of three. She sells bangles to the local customers and earns her living. When asked if she knows about the recent hijab controversy, she says the burqa makes her feel safe as nobody is able to recognize her face since it is covered.

One of the most common things on the streets of Hyderabad is Muslim women in hijab. But the hijab recently made headlines and started a fierce debate in India when six female students at a Government PU College in Udupi, Karnataka, started protesting as they were not allowed to enter classrooms wearing the hijab.

This issue garnered more attention when Hindu students started coming to colleges wearing saffron shawls, and right-wing groups on both sides started making provocative remarks. Fearing violence and tension among the students and the institution, the state government decided to shut down high schools and colleges.

Juvaria Raouf, a PhD student from Hyderabad, says for

her hijab means "to cover," a modest adornment which is used to cover women's hair, chest and half of the back. 'I view it as a sense of freedom where I allow others to see my body on my own terms and conditions,' she adds.

Yet, hijab wearing and veiling is so common in India, the recent controversy created much chaos and became a hotly debated topic and in such a scenario, it is very important to understand what hijab means to common Muslim women in India.

For Najla PV, hijab is the manifestation of her religion. She says, 'It is a visible part of my religious life. I value it very much and feel protected when I wear it. It actually works as a protection to anybody as well. You also can use a shawl or scarf to cover your face and head while driving or going outside to protect yourself from the dust and heat.'

The hijab debate is complex and opens doors to new forms of debates worldwide.

PV adds that as far as she knows there are forbidden body parts for both men and women according to Islam. There are women who choose to wear the burqa which covers both head and face, while other women choose to only wear hijab, a head covering, mostly a scarf that covers only the hair. 'The practice of religion differs from person to person but there is always a standard form of religion, I cover my head not my face,' she says.

In a country like India, where different forms of religion, culture and traditions exist simultaneously, the right to express one's own opinion and ideas is often not well-received. Now what makes it more complicated? Most women are mostly concerned about their safety.

Aleema is concerned for her safety. She says it is her burqa that makes her feel comfortable and secure when most of the shops are run by men. 'I wear the burqa because it is in Islam, also somewhere I feel it protects me from the unwanted male gaze. I am able to do my daily chores as I am not conscious of who is looking at me as my face is covered,' says Rushda Shaheen.

Massarat Fatima, a student in Hyderabad says that for her hijab is a sign of modesty. It is a personal choice and thinks that it is simply a piece of clothing that covers the wider areas of the human body.

There is no doubt that the recent hijab controversy is now discussed openly and mostly among the students in India. The constructed idea of hijab wearing women as oppressed and subjugated isn't acceptable to Fatima who says, 'The misconception about hijab is that it suppresses women. It subjugates and confines her freedom. But it does not. It has not stopped me from becoming successful or limited me in any way. One can cover oneself while still carrying out many duties. Rather, it enables me to do more as it protects me from objectification. It is a sense of security from the mindset of people who sexualize women's bodies by seeing the kind of attire they choose to wear.'

For many Muslim women students, hijab does not cover one's mind or intellect, and it is her freedom to choose what to wear and how to wear it. But it cannot be negated that Karnataka's recent hijab row has created an environment of hatred within the student community. Also, for many it's an open attack on minorities in India.

Aaminah Shaikh opines that the ban on hijab violates the religious freedom granted to minorities under the Constitution of India and its continuance is simply an attack on secularism and religious freedom.

'The ban itself is one part of the planned targeting and

attacks on Muslim symbols and practices by the Right-wing parties. Their aim is to impose majoritarian values on Indian minorities, polarize the society and create a vote-bank for themselves. The subsequent anti-hijab protests that spread throughout the state were not at all spontaneous, but a calculated ploy by the Right-wing Hindutva parties to mobilize the students based on communal polarization and bigotry,' says Shaikh.

Juvaria further argues and questions the government about why it sees the hijab as so controversial. She says, 'Hijab is just a piece of cloth used to cover. If its use gives people the audacity to question an individual's personal choice then I don't think this society is going in the right direction. The government over there has turned a personal choice of women to a heckling row. This only makes the voice loud and clear that if you are a woman your choice will be questioned, if you are a minority your rights are at risk.'

She adds, 'As a general notion we girls tend to cover ourselves in summers to protect ourselves from sun-tan. Then can I say that they too are hijabis. Just because hijab is an Arabic term to cover so ban the minority women from doing it. If it would have been a mandatory part of the majoritarian culture of this country then what would be the paradigm?'

This isn't the first time when the hijab has made the headlines in India. It cannot be denied that educational institutions are now polarized, and where religion and education do not appear to be going hand in hand.

Najla strongly opines that the hijab ban in Karnataka is absolutely absurd and illogical and it has nothing to do with so called "uniformity" and it is another articulation of the "fascist regime" ruling our country. With these kinds of actions from the government, secularist ideas are in an existential crisis. The right to education of Muslim women is under great threat. It can be seen as a well-planned attack on Muslims in general and Muslim women in particular to gradually block their educational progress and growth which they have struggled to attain so far.

She further adds, 'It is literally terrifying to watch school/ college students become rivals of their classmates. I don't understand why people don't think, and accept the political agenda behind this which is highly visible. Why are people blinded about the realities happening around them? I become more pessimistic when I think about it. I remember when our Kashmiri Muslim friends warned us that the fascism there in Kashmir would soon come and knock at our door as well. And yes now it's here at our doorsteps, spread all over India.'

She even shares her experience that personally she has never encountered any attack because she wears the hijab. She added that some friends had asked her to remove her hijab, out of curiosity, which she declined with due respect and they backed down and even apologized later for making such a request of her.

As the situation is worsened by provocative statements, it is definitely going to affect Muslim women who wear hijabs in educational spaces. Yusra (name changed on request) thinks that things are not going in the right direction. When most of the girls are fighting with their family to pursue higher education in India, such a scenario curtails their right to education. Education is the key to women's emancipation and it is not possible unless they are encouraged to pursue it. Such cases actually throw light on how any woman in India struggles to go to college, especially in contexts where they are stopped just in the name of the attire they choose to wear. The agency is now given to certain people in society to decide what is appropriate and what is not. She says, 'What is more important to the government? My hijab or my future?'

Aaminah also firmly believes that education teaches one to respect each other's religious thoughts. She says, 'I strongly feel that my hijab elevates me in status. I have chosen to submit to my Creator and not to his creation and I am deeply proud of this. If anyone feels that a Muslim girl's hijab signifies oppression and bondage, they are deeply mistaken because the reality is the contrary. My hijab frees me from submission to others to satisfy their baser needs. For me it is a revolt against the crass consumerism of the flesh.'

As the situation escalated in recent months, it is quite evident that it is now not easy to separate religion from education. It would be unwise to say that it has garnered more political and religious mileage rather than being a debate centred on educational institutions. As the responses in this piece show, this debate is more multi-faceted, complex and intertwined. The hijab debate is geopolitical, and brings identity politics into the discussions. While the issue is sensitive in itself, the significance of this debate is more international than just limiting it to Karnataka in India. Therefore, it is important to know how educational institutions are now visibly changing and permit greater cultural assertion, while asking if this row focuses on education to all. It is now obvious that secularist ideas are under question, and the hijab ban is more of a political tool to undermine the future of many students whose larger aim is to pursue higher education.

References

Arya, Divya. "Karnataka hijab controversy is polarising its classrooms." 2022. https://www.bbc.com/news/world-asia-india-60384681

M.S., Sreeja. "Explained: Karnataka Hijab Row And Timeline Of Events." 2022. https://www.ndtv.com/india-news/explained-karnataka-hijab-row-and-timeline-of-events-2774140

Pedersen. Hvass Gry. "The Role of Islam in Muslim Higher Education in India: The Case of Jamia Millia Islamia in New Delhi." *Review of Middle East Studies*, vol. 50, no. 1, pp. 28-37.

Winter, Bronwyn. "The Great Hijab Coverup." *Off Our Backs*, vol. 36, no. 3, 2006, pp. 38-40.

HIJABOPHOBIA IN KERALA

Some Reflections

J. Devika

Like most other irrational fears, "hijabophobia" in Kerala is uniquely Malayali. "Malayali" refers to the popular sense of cultural belonging to Kerala as a place and Malayalam as a language, and it relatively recent in Indian history. This was because the three areas where Malayalam was spoken predominantly were politically separate until 1957, when the Kerala State was formed. Kerala State was formed as a long campaign in which reformed upper-caste social groups and their culture gained prominence. Christians and Muslims were assigned supporting roles in this discourse, commended for not aspiring to political power and submitting to insertion into the order of caste defended by political power in Malayalam-speaking regions. In post-independence Kerala, the Muslim community, despite its obvious aspirations to modernity, continued to be treated as a symbol of backwardness and irrationality.

Contemporary Malayali hijabophobia draws on all this. The great leaps made by the Malayali Muslim community in education after the migration to the Gulf countries since the early 1970s remains less visible in mainstream sensibilities; however, the transformations in Muslim religious architecture, housing, sartorial styles, and consumption in general have been under hostile scrutiny. Mid-20th century prejudice is now mapped on to unfolding 21st century scenarios. For instance, post-Babri Masjid Muslim political formations are too readily dubbed irrational, "backward," and anti-modern; new veiling practices are treated as evidence of the worsening of women's freedoms among Muslims, with no consideration at all for the fact that Muslim women have entered into higher education in unprecedented numbers and have made significant gains in all sectors of education, in public life, and employment now. This hijabophobia makes no substantial difference between the many different styles of veiling that early-21st century Malayali Muslim women have adopted—at best, the mafta and the niqab may be identified with different degrees of submission.

Hijabophobia in Kerala, as must be evident by now, is not an exclusively hindu or Hindutva tendency; it rests on Kerala's claims to high social development and the alleged reluctance of the Muslim community to participate in "modern" (in Malayali parlance, "Navoddhana" or "Renaissance") values. It views with suspicion any sartorial code that is explicitly religious and inseparable from religious identity, but singles out Muslim styles, especially female styles, as fear-inducing. It also conflates patriarchy among the Muslim community which puts greater pressure on women to accept religious dressing with veiling itself, as though the exposure of the female body were an automatic indicator of women's freedom.

An interesting variant of Malayali hijabophobia, however, looks back nostalgically to Muslim women's traditional dressing style, popularized especially in Malayalam cinema, arguing that the issue with the late-twentieth and early twenty-first century veiling practices is not that they are religious or patriarchal, but foreign—drawn from (anti-liberal, non-democratic) Saudi Arabian Islam. The face-covering niqab particularly is perceived as contrary to an ostensibly "open" Malayali ethos, signifying cultural allegiance to not Kerala but Saudi Arabia.

II

Perhaps the first step towards exposing these sentiments as manifestations of Islamophobia and not simply concern for ostensibly-pristine and purely-indigenous "Malayali culture" is to historicize the very idea of "Malayali" as well as contest the indigenity of its constituents. This has been ably done by many historians of Kerala in a broader context in which the leftist national-popular which undergirded 20th century Malayali sub-nationalism unravelled steadily since the mid-1980s—especially with the self-assertions of social groups fully or partially excluded from this sub-national imaginary, or instrumentalized to its ends (for example, "Malayali women," who have been both invisible and hypervisible in the discourse of Kerala as social development paradise).

Here I want to dwell upon two claims of Malayali hijabophobia that seem to have received relatively less scholarly attention: the claim that the recent practices of veiling among Malayali Muslim women are an implicit rejection of indigenous Malayali identity, and that they are evidence for intensifying of Muslim patriarchal control on Muslim women. As hypotheses, these are not easy to test in empirical research; the sheer limitations of the

survey method and interview-based methods make it hard
to obtain conclusive results for either. Besides, it may be
crucial to ask how and why they figure, in the first place,
as hypotheses. For example, why is it that we do not ask
if the saree, undoubtedly, cultural import to Kerala of the
twentieth century, or the salwar-kameez, or the ubiquitous
house gown ("nightie" in contemporary Malayalam) incites
Malayali cultural anxiety around foreignness? And though
we know perfectly well that all these items of female
clothing are acceptable precisely under the terms of Malayali
mainstream patriarchy, why is that discomfort not a source
of fear, as it is with the abaya? Though both the hindu
head-and-face covering ghoonghat and the Muslim niqab
are both relatively unfamiliar in Kerala, why is the former
exoticized and associated with romance, while the latter is
demonized? In short, why does the abaya/mafta/hijab/niqab/
burqa alone carry the burden of foreignness and patriarchy?

Reflecting on the differing histories of the saree and
Muslim women's dress might help to clarify some of these
questions. The modern saree popularized throughout regions
in India during the twentieth century, it is now well-known,
was an invention of the modern educated Indian elite in
Bombay and Bengal during the nineteenth century, who
were in close proximity with colonial authorities, and that
it was further reformed to fit the ideal of the reformed
Indian woman as imagined by the various strands of elite
social reformisms in various parts of the subcontinent.
Indeed, additions like the corset-like "blouse" and the
petticoat brought it in line with the European gown. In
the Malayalam-speaking regions, the uncovered breasts of
women posed a tremendous challenge to local claims to be
a "civilized" society in the eyes of the colonial authorities,

missionaries, and the modern-educated elite. A variant of the saree combining the upper cloth, blouse, and the mundu (waist cloth) began to be used among educated circles in the late nineteenth century, popularized especially by female missionary educators. This was different from the combinations of these three items of clothing already prevalent here but did not displace traditional combinations immediately. For example, Syrian Christian women in the 1920s continued to wear the traditional chatta-mundu-kavani (blouse-waist cloth-upper cloth) in high school and college, and often moved to the saree only when they took up public employment or office—as recalled by Anna Chandy, feminist intellectual and the first woman lawyer from the Malayalam-speaking regions, in her autobiography. The saree, despite being cumbersome and unsuited to the heat and long, wet monsoons in the region, despite it being high-maintenance clothing, and despite the deeply patriarchal discourses in which it was ensconced, was accepted as the symbol of social upward mobility. It is no coincidence that the elite embraced it, for it is they who could afford it. The combination of the upper cloth, mundu, and blouse emerged as the "traditional" version of the saree long before the off-white "Kerala saree" popular in contemporary times—and they often defined "work wear" and "home wear" respectively for elite women. Women of the former oppressed-caste communities who rejected traditional caste-revealing attire inevitably wore the saree as a marker of the social upward mobility that they had gained through social reform and economic mobility in the late nineteenth- early twentieth century.

In short, the saree was definitely "foreign" but soon it came to be adapted by the Malayali elite at a time when the political and cultural horizon of Malayali society was Indian nationalism. The saree and mundu-upper cloth-blouse came to be adopted soon across classes and castes despite the tediousness which reeked of patriarchy—flagged by the early Malayali feminist K Saraswathi Amma—and despite the fact that many suspected it to be too amenable to immodest draping. In the mid-twentieth century decades, the religious minorities adopted it enthusiastically. Traditional Christian and Muslim female clothing was replaced among the educated elites by the saree, and the saree was itself used in Muslim veiling, with the saree edge covering the head, waist and arms and sometimes worn with long-sleeved blouses. This style still persists among a sizeable number of Muslim women in Kerala and the shift did not evoke any fear of "foreignness." In the late-20th century however, when the numbers of women entering higher education rose and the service sector in Kerala began to register higher growth rates, providing more openings to women in employment, the salwar-kameez began to overtake the saree. However, this shift did not evoke any worries about cultural contamination (though the early name of the salwar-kameez in Kerala—"Pathan suit"—pointed to its Muslim origins). Around the same time, women's home dress shifted to what is now popularly called the nightie— the night gown—popularized here by Gulf Malayalis. The nightie, contrary to its name, was worn through day and night, as work wear and sleep wear, and perhaps "casual neighbourhood wear" too, as women found it convenient to wear on neighbourhood visits and nearby shopping trips if a towel was thrown on the breast as a gesture towards modesty. This, actually, made it come quite close to the abaya. While the nightie and women's preference for this garment has excited much derision, sarcasm, and even contempt (on the charge that it was ugly and shapeless on the one hand, and often too revealing and immodest without the towel, on the other), it definitely provoked no fear of cultural loss. And far from being criticized as a tool of patriarchy, in some instances, especially in feminist discussions, the masculine disapproval of the nightie was read as evidence for its power to obstruct the male gaze.

In short, the modern saree was "foreign," cumbersome, and clearly accepted under the terms of modern patriarchy; the nightie was "foreign" too, so also the salwar-kameez, and both of these items of clothing were attributed associations, in different ways, to Muslim societies or culture. But none of them evoke the paranoia that the abaya seems to evoke. These would be "foreign" in the sense that their origins were outside Kerala—and not in the sense that it was imposed on the local people by invaders or colonisers. All these were choices made by women, sometimes in defiance of family or community authorities, even though they were all clearly serving the ends of patriarchy in a broader sense.

III

And what about Muslim women's dress in Kerala? First of all, the claim that the traditional kaachi-thattam-blouse (the waist-cloth—head scarf—blouse) combination being "native" or a product of "cultural assimilation" needs to be subjected to critical scrutiny.[1] For it seems to share resemblance with

---

1. A typical example of Malayali distrust of contemporary veiling practices, complete with the nostalgia for the traditional Muslim female dress style, the argument that it was a product of Muslim cultural assimilation, and the distrust of present adoption of abaya by Muslim women, the hint that this is being enforced by Muslim clerics one-sidedly,

the attire of Muslim women in many other south-east Asian Muslim communities at least as much as those of other caste-communities in the Malayalam-speaking world. The blindness to this fact is probably not surprising, given the propensity in Kerala to highlight western connections (Arab, Roman, European) via the sea over long-standing social and economic connections with South-East Asia and other parts of South Asia.

See for example, the dress of Muslim women in Malaya as portrayed by a Portuguese artist in 1540. The similarities with the traditional Muslim women's dressing style in Malabar are evident.[2] This too is not surprising, given that the Malayali Muslim community was predominantly an Indian Ocean rim community, and that a whole range of everyday objects, technologies, clothing, food, music, architecture, and skills circulated widely between Indian Ocean communities in South and South-East Asia, among both Islamic and non-Islamic communities alike well into British colonial times. There is no evidence that the "foreignness" of these was never perceived as a threat by the Hindu rulers of these regions; indeed, the Hindu communities too partook in these circulations, if one considers the significant sharing in architecture, cooking practices, and so on among the coastal societies of the Indian Ocean rim societies from Malaya to Western India at least.

In Malayan and Indonesian regions, the traditional

---

along with treating Malayali Muslim history as primarily connected with Arabia as the land of origin may be found in Panakkal, Abbas. 'To cover or not to cover'. See https://www.deccanchronicle.com/nation/current-affairs/030519/to-cover-or-not-to-cover.html

2. See https://upload.wikimedia.org/wikipedia/commons/a/af/Malays_from_the_Malacca_Sultanate_Codice_Casanatense.jpg

women's attire called baju-kurung underwent transformation and especially post-globalization in the 1990s, leading to the expansion of a global Muslim fashion market (which has drawn the attention of such scholars as Viola Thimm). In Kerala, as mentioned before, the kachi-thattam-blouse combination gave way to the saree-centred hijab in the mid-twentieth century decades among the educated Muslim middle-class. Post-globalization, Muslim women have drawn on a variety of styles, including the new hybrid styles of Malaysian and Indonesian modest fashion, as well as north Indian. The gravitation away from the saree and drawing upon styles from the West is a common trend among women of all communities, and Muslim women have been no exceptions.

This, however, coincided at a period in which Muslims were increasingly threatened with ejection from the national community in India (and Kerala). And as Caroline and Filippo Osella pointed out, the rising preference for sartorial expressions of Islamic modesty in Malabar through styles from outside the subcontinent also indexes increasing awareness of the high-Hindu roots of India's "common culture" (Osella and Osella 2007).[3] And as the processing of othering the Muslim turned increasingly intense and hostile post 9/11, so also did the distrust and disgust of Muslim women's abaya. There is every reason to believe that the increasing isolation and exclusion of the Muslim community leads to the intensification of community-patriarchal control on women and so the rising preference for the abaya may not all be women's choices. However, a rising number of young woman have articulated their preference for it, voices

---

3. Osella, Caroline, and Filippo Osella. 'Muslim Style in South India'. *Fashion Theory*, vol. 11, no. 2-3, 2007, pp. 233-52.

that cannot be dismissed. Nor can the patriarchal pressure on women of other communities to stick to decent, modest styles be ignored.

IV

Nevertheless, it appears evident from recent events that even if the Muslim woman in Kerala abandons Islamic practice altogether, she will still be excluded from high-Hindu spaces and practices, as is evident in the recent controversy about the denial of performance space to the Muslim-born dancer Mansiya VP in the premises of the Koodalmanickam temple in Irinjalakkuda.[4] Manisya has declared herself to be an atheist and is married to a Hindu man, but was denied the opportunity on the grounds that she had not converted into Hinduism. While this has led to an outcry with three dancers withdrawing from the festival in solidarity with her, the question whether the othering of the Muslim woman will end if she abandons Muslim religious dress looms large in its wake. The difficulties of accommodating such women in the Hindu fold are evident in the Vishwa Hindu Parishad's vacillation on the issue: first supporting Mansiya and offering her venues in a temple under their control, but then withdrawing in deference to conservative notions of temple custom.[5]

---

4. John, Haritha. 'Bharatanatyam dancer barred from performing in Kerala temple as she is non-Hindu'. 2022. https://www.thenewsminute. com/article/bharatanatyam-dancer-barred-performing-kerala-temple-she-non-hindu-162352.

5. See, 'Dropped by Left-controlled temple, ex-Muslim dancer gets VHP invite to perform'. https://www.mangalorean.com/dropped-by-left-controlled-temple-ex-muslim-dancer-gets-vhp-invite-to-perform/; https://malayalam.oneindia.com/news/kerala/vp-mansiya-dance-issue-viswa-hindu-parishad-said-will-not-support-mansiya-dance-over-temple-per-332960.html.

Perhaps the way out lies in forging common fronts against the Hindutva state's explicit push towards "secular" visibilities in public spaces, and its less-explicit but very real moral policing of women's dress codes in the interest of "tradition", "modesty", or "decency" in general. The fact that the hostility against Muslim women's religious dress and the moral outrage against "revealing clothing" chosen by women are both directly or indirectly fomented by the un-civil society of Hindutva (or the more silent Hindu majoritarian positions) and abetted to various degrees by the state is telling indeed. The Kiss of Love protests in Kerala in 2015 had provided an opening for reflections on such a dialogue against the moral policing of bodies and about the struggles against the state's effort to control and regulate the visibility of bodies in public spaces. However, secular liberals and the Islamists remain too divided in Kerala to see such potential. Indeed, the sad fact that it is the disunity of the oppressed, much more than the power of the oppressors, that is destroying social amity and the prospect of social conviviality in India seems reaffirmed here too.

VEILING/UNVEILING

Ambarien Alqadar

One of my earliest childhood memories is that of my mother getting down from a train in Azamgarh, Uttar Pradesh. My family was living in Aligarh at the time and my younger brother and me were on our summer vacation visit to our grandmother. In all these years I have not forgotten how my mother opened her handbag and pulled out her two-piece burqa and slipped it on with the same ease she wore a saree when she went to teach in Aligarh. My mother's burqa was green. Since then, her many transformations have told me a story of what it means to be a good daughter in a Muslim home.

My mother, Asifa Jahan Naiyer, was the first woman in her family to go to school. This was not easy for her as Sultanpur, the village where she grew up did not have a school for girls at the time. My grandparents were skeptical of her decision to follow her brother to Kanpur who was studying medicine at the time. The thought of an unmarried daughter leaving her mother's home to seek higher education was unthinkable at the time and my grandparents were fearful how she might become "modern." When I asked her to explain the term, she said it was perhaps their fear that she would be disconnected from her roots. So, my mother made a pact. This involved that she will wear a burqa in public places at all times.

My uncle, who wanted to support my mother's decision to empower herself through formal education, arranged a chauffeur-driven ambassador car that would pick her up and drop her off. My mother recalls how the car had a beautiful net curtain suspended between her and her driver in addition to her own burqa. On those trips she sometimes would take her niqab off and suspend herself outside the window in the breeze when the road was less crowded and no one was watching. Sometimes her friends joined her and they went on road trips. 'Burqa protects you from the male gaze,' she told me when I asked her the question while recording an interview with her for a work in progress film.

The few pictures I have from my childhood are those of my mother posing with me in bell bottoms by the Mediterranean Sea. My father had taken up a teaching assignment in Tripoli, Libya and they made friends with his colleagues who were from all parts of the world. My mother hosted tea parties, dinners and poetry readings and wanted to be seen as a secular Indian Muslim. I asked her why in those pictures she did not wear her burqa and she told me that it was important for her to claim her Indianness as part of being a secular Muslim. She wanted to let her friends know through her subtle choices of what she wore and what she chose not to, that as an Indian Muslim she had the choice in deciding how she presented herself to the world. She was proud of how Indian Muslims could choose how they defined themselves and often those choices involved navigating the fluid possibilities in the everyday.

In 1984 my family relocated to New Delhi, India and

my father built our home in Jamia Nagar, New Delhi. My mother talks of how she felt comfortable and secure in a neighborhood where a Muslim way of life came to surround her. The azaan, the morning call to prayer, reminded her of her childhood. It was the kind of comfort she had missed for a long time. The Friday afternoon Namaz on the streets, the smell of biryani and itr, the Eid market and the Ramzan night celebrations were all things she had missed while trying to live as a secular Muslim. She had grown tired of hiding her way of life and spiritual practice that made her feel grounded and connected to her roots. She often spoke of how her sense of security in Jamia Nagar stemmed from remembering what happened in Hashimpura in 1987, Bhagalpur in 1989, Mumbai in 1992 and Gujarat in 2002. The timeline of these events was interspersed with constant reminders of how she found a new kind of freedom and mobility in Jamia Nagar. As the riots happened in Gujarat 2002, she opened a beauty salon as a place where women like her could find care and community. As part of this, she also wrapped and folded those red and pink bell-bottoms into an attic in our home, started covering her hair and became more "Muslim." In 2012 while filming 'The Ghetto Girl' I found the bell-bottoms folded and wrapped with care in muslin in a suitcase.

As part of growing up in Jamia Nagar I had to negotiate two worlds—one for which I was never Muslim enough and one where I was too Muslim. I used to be called a ghetto girl at the Roman Catholic school I went to. My address and name carried a weight and I fought hard to resist it but at the same time there was the fight to be able to wear jeans back home. I was in 8th grade when my father told me it was the last time I could wear it. I remember how my mother had bought a deep blue denim pair with big red buttons to wear to a school end year party. Colourful clothes day at school became a source of deep anguish for me as everyone wore short skirts and jeans and I had to wear a salwar-kameez. The size of my school skirt and for most of us from Jamia Nagar reached our ankles but sure we found a way to work around it we folded our skirts at the waist once we got onto the school bus and became the "modern" women in ways our parents perhaps did not want us to become.

In college my parents told me that I had to wear a hijab. I was a rebel by the time. I had arguments with my parents about the place of women in Islam and unlike my extended family where critical questioning of Islam is blasphemy, my parents gave me the courage and confidence to question. Sometimes there was heartbreak on both sides. Like the one time my mother discovered that I was actually taking off my hijab on my way to college. We had an argument and it was in making my case for freedom within Islam, that I became myself. I constructed my argument from examples of women in Islam such as Hazrat Khadija, Hazrat Ayesha and Bibi Halima and also from my radical reading of Nisa, the chapter in Quran that translates as "woman." I argued that the text called for modesty and not for a piece of cloth. I chose to not wear the hijab and my parents' difficult love found a way to support me. The fight one wages in the intimate sphere of the family is most often invisible, nevertheless for me it has been the hardest fight.

In 2015 I relocated to US seeking personal freedom. Having to lay down my own roots as an immigrant forced my own history and me to reconsider who I was. In that was buried the question of where I belonged. Long days of homesickness were punctuated by brief calm when I recreated my mother's recipes and her rituals. She sent me Eid wishes and birthday cards reminding me to pray and be a good Muslim. In 2017 she visited me and wanted to go to a local mosque for Eid prayers. I covered my head, just as she did and joined her. Distance gave me the lens to relook at my mother and understand that the space she gave me to disagree with her, question her belief systems and make my own case for freedom was also part of the love she had for me. Freedom in that sense is an ability to choose how one defines being Muslim. In that sense one woman's right to wear the hijab is as valuable as another's right to question it.

PART FOUR

MANY
FEMINISMS

HIJAB: TO BE OR NOT TO BE

Noor Zaheer

I am not quite sure how many times I heard the story. It was a story I wanted to hear again and again. Strangely enough, the story became, if possible, more engrossingly fascinating with each retelling. The reason my mother, a child of eight, was made to wear the burqa. Razia Dilshad, a girl of eight, had written and posted a story in the children's magazine *Phool* published from Lahore. The editor had accepted the story and sent a line of encouragement. The postcard landed in the hands of her paternal grandfather, who declared that the family's honour had been tarnished and the only way to reclaim it was to confine the child of eight year to purdah.

Three of her short stories, written much later in life, voice the anguish, humiliation and captivity of characters restricted to purdah with their agency for making any contribution to society snatched away on the excuse of saving the family honour or adherence to the directives of the religion.

The story however continued and I heard in awe my mother narrating the events of the third night after her arranged marriage with my father when he suggested that she give up burqa. She was astute enough to ask the reason for such a proposition. He had provided two: she was a woman and that was nothing to be ashamed of; he was not her owner; they were comrades and had to do loads of work for the independence of the country; burqa hid her identity and would be a hindrance in work. Next day the new burqa, made specially for the bride's trousseau was thrown away.

Every time, at the end of the story, I would gaze in awe at Ammi who never covered her head, grateful that my sisters or I never had to wear burqa.

It was only when I was 18 and my father had been dead for three years that I asked Ammi, how she, a girl brought up in the strict discipline of Islam and confined to purdah from the age of eight immediately accepted Abba's suggestion to give it up? Her answer was simple: It was an opportunity. I didn't wish to miss it. Suppose it never arose again?

That is the crux of the matter. Make most of the opportunity while it is available and move forward with it. Denial, self-imposed or forced, can never be a right. But many women will put forward this argument that it is their way of proclamation of womanhood.

In the first year in college, me and Mahjabeen formed a strong bond because of our dislike for purdah. We made fun of 'hoodies', girls who wore the hijab but not the naqab, pointing out new, gold and silver embroidered burqas and laughed at the pride some felt for burqas sent from the middle east by a caring relative. Mahjabeen was married off while she was still in college and moved to Canada. We reconnected some twenty years later when I visited Toronto. I was a few minutes late for the appointment and was walking briskly when I stopped dead in my tracks. A woman clad head to toe in a black burqa was waving and calling out my name. It couldn't be Mahjabeen and if it was, her husband was a dead man. That is what everyone assumes—that it is the man who has forced the woman to don the burqa. I was wrong. The first thing the fellow said to me was, 'Can you please convince Mahjabeen to give up purdah? Everyone presumes that I have forced my wife to wear it.' Deep into the night, having exhausted news of the past, we came to the topic that both of us knew we would. Mahajabeen's reasoning was simple, 'Nobody noticed me before. Now everyone says, oh the solicitor in a hijab.'

'But then, Mahjabeen, isn't it exhibitionism? Why is only exposing one's body exhibitionism; doesn't this amount to the same? Dressing in a manner to attract attention.' She calmed down after an initial burst of anger and we discussed that if we oppose a woman showing off her body in the name of commodification, then isn't this just another kind of marketing? One is obviously not confident of making a mark through education and intelligence to adapt this superficial change to attract attention.

I am not for giving up on purdah on the plea that it is not part of the five tenets of Islam: Faith in one Allah and His Prophet, Namaz, Roza, Haj and Zakaat. Nor do I buy the argument that Hijab protects women, that a woman in burqa is respected. Women clad from head to toe in black are equally "eve-teased," molested, misbehaved with. One has to only discuss this with girls in Muslim-run institutions, witness the crowd of hooligans outside girls' schools and find out the number of dropouts from Muslim girls' schools. Women have to understand that no religion stands for women. And I say this about all religions, the one that binds her to a man for seven births (a Brahmanical Hindu idea now accepted commonly by most believing north Indian Hindus), or the one who gives her the right to enter a contract of marriage but none to come out of it. The so-called reformist movements within Islam, the Ismaili or Bohri or Qadaiyani, have restricted the woman further. Besides all the religions and their diktats, that make much of how prohibited they are to the woman, they have to be understood in the context of the deep patriarchy that exists in three-fourths of the world.

Young girls, (in fact all the youth, but that is another discussion) are at the mercy of the elders who decide the kind of school, the subjects in college, the time she returns home, the friends she makes, the boy to marry and the list is endless. True financial circumstances also force the hands of the family to send their girls to a madrasa or a public school. But often it is adherence to the norms set by patriarchy that inform these decisions.

Zarina and her sisters were students at the Loreto Convent in Lucknow. Her family lived in the government quarters in central Lucknow, where walls did not divide the backyard and the front space. The women often gathered in the backyard to gossip, the men brought out chairs to sit on the front porch and the girls moved freely visiting friends in the neighborhood. Returning from a neighbour's house Zarina had salaamed her father's friends, little realizing that her head was uncovered. The men, however, could not ignore such a big blunder. Her father had been so ashamed that a mere scolding and apology from the girl was not enough to calm his fuming rage. Next day, 13-year-old Zarina was removed from the convent school and put in a Muslim girls' school. A typical patriarchal response and punishment.

Ismat Chughtai, in her autobiography, writes about this

in detail. As a young girl, supported by her elder brother, Azeem Beg Chughtai (a well-known Urdu writer in his own right), Ismat decided not to wear a burqa on a visit to her paternal home in Agra. The two men, an uncle and a cousin, who had come to receive her, were so embarrassed, that they turned heel and ran away from the station, leaving a young girl alone to negotiate her way to the house. So, it was not the woman showing her face or moving in public with an uncovered head who was ashamed, it was the men. While it was a conscious decision for her to not be ashamed of her identity, for the patriarchal society it was a matter of prestige. A woman moving around freely meant that the men of her family had no control over the women.

Women, who are today standing up for the freedom of women to wear or not wear the hijab, have to understand that the breaking of the code of conduct brings "shame" to the men and decide if they are happy with the this "power-game" where they have the responsibility of protecting the family honour but no right to decide what would bring shame to it.

The most important issue here is the financial and social dependence of the female on the male. A large number of girls who did not wear any extra covering during school opt for wearing a hijab in college/university. Many of them do this so they can educate themselves and hopefully become independent. Society has not managed so far to build any kind of a haven where a woman questioning the norms of patriarchy can find refuge.

While no safe haven for a rebel is available there are those who insist that burqa is a safe space. That a woman is free, when she is obscured by an outer cover. A short play in a Muslim girls' school demonstrated this belief. A young girl, tied up in chains was brought to the stage (with much heaving and pushing, poor thing). The audience was asked if they thought the girl was free? The reply was in the negative and then another actor walked up, unchained her and put a burqa on her. "And now?" came the pointed question which received the answer in affirmative accompanied with much clapping for the burqa that sets a woman free. The narrator went on to elaborate, a woman in burqa is so free that she can even eye the men without the men knowing it. Restricted is the poor man who has to make do with eyeing just the burqa. Nobody points out the few seconds when the girl was unchained, not covered up in black, and was really free.

A professor of Allahabad said wistfully in a public gathering, how she wished her religion allowed her to wear a naqab, elaborating that it would be her own safe space. Why was she so happy with such a limited space? And if that is what she wanted, why didn't she just do it? Half the girls walking in the summer sun, don head and face cover to protect their complexion. Nobody wonders if they have converted to Islam? Why is a person's superficial display associated with their religious identity? When one looks at this objectively, it stands out for what it is—a proclamation of one's community. Look a little further and see the variety in the Hijab—all announcing sects, factions and cults: a Wahabi Muslim, a Bohri one, or Memon, Khoja, Shia. Not only should a woman announce that she is a Muslim when she steps out of her house, she should also broadcast the group/division she belongs to.

In a lighter vein but with serious consequence is the confusion that burqas can cause. Women all seem the same in black. This often results in much older women but of slim figure, bearing the brunt of catcalls, love calls and "eve-teasing." Almost every woman in her fifties has a story when she was the target of a man much younger than her, who walked, cycled, drove following her, reciting love couplets, singing bawdy songs and calling for a glimpse of her face; till the woman fed up of simply ignoring him, decided to turn, show her face, call him "son" and shame him.

Girls often exchange burqas. With the gulf countries demanding fitting, laced and embroidered hijabs and the fashion industry exploiting the lucrative market that it presents, hijab is a style statement. The variety available in the market has girls wearing the best they can afford. Exchanging to try out a different one is usual. Brothers have been known to recognize the burqa of their sister, and tease the friend, when indeed it was their own sister in a different burqa.

In Iran women are giving up the hijab and moving around without a head covering in protest against the gender bias in the law that demands that a woman wear hijab. Moral policing is common in Iran. They are stopped, heckled and harassed, even arrested. But instead of being intimidated they use their phones to record the "eve teasers", women questioning the men who remind them to wear veils, and of arrests by law enforcers. The religion of these women is not threatened and it is time women across the world realize that the actual fight is about gender equality which can never be won by gender segregation.

The struggle for gender equality has to be fought across class and communities. A very strong reason for believing this is the Indian Constitution which in its very Preamble promises equality to all citizens of India. This equality is ours to take, so why don't the Muslim women use what has been guaranteed by the Constitution and will help us win our rights and freedom on the streets and in our families.

On the international scene, the right-wing presidential candidate of France who has just been defeated was hell bent on "removing" hijabis from public space. No questions were asked of how doing this would help the rising living cost, failing economy of France or for that matter the western world. Would it even help sort out the war taking place between the two white communities in Europe? The British Prime Minister is on record calling hijab-clad Muslim women "letter boxes." On the flip side, in Bahrain, a British restaurant manager, apparently of Indian Hindu descent stopped a woman in hijab from entering the café. He was probably trying to please his ultra-right saffron brigade masters. He has since been suspended, shall probably lose his job and head back to India, where he would be treated as a hero. Why should this scum of the earth become a hero? The right-wing everywhere and more so in the developing countries, tries to use these tactics to divert attention of the masses from the real issues of economic growth, development and social welfare. Humiliating one section of the society is meant to give a sense of "feel good" to the other sections. While this kind of humiliation and nonchalant rightwing appeasement should never be a deciding factor for giving up something that one really wants to do, it can be used as the initiation of a discussion within the community. A much-needed churning to evaluate the necessity of sticking to archaic practices.

The Muslim community and their sympathizers in the other communities should set higher, more difficult goals for themselves than wearing or not wearing a form of dress.

As an example, I would speak of the under-representation of Muslims in the security and armed forces, the attack on Muslim social and cultural leaders for voicing the indignity and threats the community is constantly faced with and the insignificant presence of Muslim women in sports. Here it is important to recall the humiliation Sania Mirza, the Tennis player was subjected to, by the right wingers from both sides. The Muslim fundamentalists criticizing her for wearing a short skirt while on the court, not ever wearing a hijab, participating in a fashion show once and making a statement about her tennis being more important than fasting during Ramadan. The Hindu saffron brigade was equally critical of her saying Namaz before a game, giving credit to her parents for praying for her during Hajj as she played and won the Junior Wimbledon, and on her choice of partner, a Pakistani sports person.

Women never have it easy. It has and shall continue to be a struggle every inch of the way of existence. But to struggle is proof that one is human, to fight on is to be. Everyone needs a fight to subsist. The fatwa giving maulvi, the patriarchal father, the possessive male, has no fight in his life. So, he builds up these fights within the community. The women, the patriarchal set up believes, are weak and so need men in all forms, including as religious heads, to protect them. Or maybe not provide the protection; they are there to create fear. Any believer will proudly say that he is "God fearing." This terror of 'life after death' dictates whatever one does in 'life on earth.' A woman, incidentally the initiator of the "original sin," has to be controlled and kept within limits that have been decided by religion and the sins she commits shall decide her punishment or rewards in the afterlife.

The conclusion is with the three-line story of Rabia, said to be the first female Sufi. She was once seen on the road carrying a bucket of embers and a pail of water. When asked what she was intending to do, she replied that with the embers she wished to burn the rewards of Paradise and with the water she wished to douse the fires of hell, so that nobody worshipped Allah for fear of burning in Hell, or for the incentives of Heaven. People would then worship God for the love of him.

Giving up on hijab/naqab, is merely overcoming the fear of the vengeance patriarchy can vent on the ones whom it labels "rebels." The conformists do not attempt or succeed in changing the world. Whatever is happening in the name of hijab, is, one way or another a means to terrorize a community through its women. The onus of not being frightened, to turn around and face the stalker is the only way to overcome this fear.

'CAN'T A SCARF BE PART OF A UNIFORM?'

Nuancing Feminist Critique of Culture Politics

Ghazala Jamil

Garments have often been used to signal or announce politics across history and time. Consider, for example, the changing and varied symbolisms of Khadi. Various political organisations have cultures of dressing in a particular way—certain fabrics and certain garments are seen as more acceptable and appropriate. In activist circles, dressing up deliberately in inexpensive fabrics or garments, which might be considered "shabby" in other settings, is quite common. Whether these norms are articulated clearly or not they are enforced through sub-cultural peer pressure.

The young Muslim girl students had been attending school wearing scarves, causing no harm to anyone, nor any disruption in the classroom. Groups of boys started wearing saffron stoles as a pressure tactic and forced school administrations to tell the Muslim girls to take off their scarves if they wanted to enter the classrooms. It needs to be probed as to what was it that bothered the boys exactly?

On the face of it, the sporting of saffron stoles, blocking gates, and aggressive sloganeering amounted to bullying with a sole intent to harass and humiliate these girls. Instead of resolving this issue in a manner that allowed the girls to continue their education, the school administration and state government acted in a manner that emboldened the boys and disrupted the girls' education. That this issue was raked up in the middle of the academic year shows the move to be malafide, rather than being a routine administrative process and in response to vigilante groups. Karnataka High Court too provided no relief. The bench, instead of taking up the issue within the framework of right to education, treated the case as a test of wearing of scarf/hijab as an Essential Religious Practice (ERP). The manner in which the keenly watched hearings were conducted made it very clear that it was going to follow the well-established pattern in India that any dispute that involves Muslims as one party gets framed as a controversy about Islam. The KHC bench neglected to examine the matter from any other possible points of view—foremost among them could have been the important matter of education and protection from arbitrary administrative action. However it chose to examine the issue from the point of view of ERP, even as the bigger question on this issue remains pending before a 9-judge bench at the Supreme Court of India in the Sabarimala case.[1]

Could the legal question simply have been, 'Can't a scarf be part of a uniform?'

Which garments are considered most appropriate in

---

1. TNN, 'Hijab row: Focus back on Sabarimala case pending before SC.' *The Times of India*, March 16. 2022. https://timesofindia.indiatimes.com/india/hijab-row-focus-back-on-sabarimala-case-pending-before-sc/articleshow/90243976.cms.

which context may be deeply contested but those who are extolling the virtues of uniforms might consider that uniforms can be tools of control too and students in colleges do experience not having to wear uniforms as freedom. Clothes can also express resistance to forms of oppression. Clearly, restriction on clothing is political.

Clothing is a primal, physiological and emotional human response to environment. Indeed, archaeologists are beginning to unearth evidence that it was not food that triggered the evolutionary and civilisational response of taking up agriculture and settling down, but clothing.[2] The way wearers experience a particular garment is contextual. All garments acquire contextual meaning. There is no inherent meaning fixed into any garment.

Across history, garments in one region have also been influenced by norms and fashions of other cultures. This is because of cultural exchange and influence of trade, colonialism, and, more recently, globalisation. We only have to look at the dominant fashion for men across the world today to understand the influence of these processes. But women are considered repositories of national or community cultures more than men and their garments are mandated to put this on display. Covering of the head is a norm in

---

2. The role of late Pleistocene climate changes necessitating the use of clothing and hence the evolution of modern human behaviour has been studied. See Gilligan, Ian. 'Clothing and Modern Human Behaviour: Prehistoric Tasmanic as a case study.' *Archaeology in Oceania*, vol. 42, no. 4, 2013, pp. 102-111. The study of formation of culture by Neandertals, thus predating its origins from the time of early Homo Sapiens, by looking at clothing has also been done. See for details, Burdukiewicz, Jan Michał. 'The Origin of Symbolic Behavior of Middle Palaeolithic Humans: Recent Controversies.' *Quaternary International*, vol. 326-327, 2014, pp. 398-405. For a more accessible articulation of this argument by Gilligan see https://aeon.co/essays/how-clothing-and-climate-change-kickstarted-agriculture.

many cultures. If one looks at the Islamic countries across Africa and Asia, it is easy to notice a diversity of norms of what is acceptable and fashionable.

Could Hijab have not been made a part of the uniform? Boys and girls usually have different uniforms, Girls wear skirts or tunics with collared shirts or wear salwar kameez, some schools require a dupatta over it, or and boys mostly wear trousers or shorts. Winter uniforms are different from summer uniforms in many parts of the country depending on the local climate. If "Beti Bachao, Beti Padhao" is not an empty slogan then the governments in question should take a serious look at their complete failure to take steps to protect Muslim women from male aggression in government schools and colleges. The disbarment of Muslim girl students is not the first instance when minority cultural rights are under question and a simple question of civic rights has been turned into a controversy about Islam and Muslim Personal Law.

In a study conducted by NUEPA it was found that between the academic years 2007-8 and 2011-12 Muslim enrolment increased at a very fast pace. This was especially striking because during the same period there was stagnation in overall enrolment in the country. In primary classes Muslim children's enrollment went up by 25% and in middle school it went up by 50%. On the whole, for classes I to VIII, Muslim students' enrolment in this period saw a rise of 31%. While the national increase was just 4%.[3] The figures of Muslim girls' enrolment were even better—26%

---

3. Rampal, Nikhil. '"Muslims" enrolment in higher education rises by 37%, gender parity also improves.' *The Print*, 29 July 2018. https://theprint.in/india/governance/muslims-enrolment-in-higher-education-rises-by-37-gender-parity-also-improves/90152/.

in primary, 54% in upper primary (33% increase in class I to VIII against 5% national average).[4] Even after this period the trend has been of a steady uptick in these figures.[5]

It is against the backdrop of these encouraging trends that the latest vigilante campaigns to stop scarf-wearing Muslim students from attending schools and getting an education, must be contextualised. Further and more importantly, this article seeks to nuance the feminist stances on the culture politics of women's garments and their education.

Whether and which religious mandates to follow, and to what degree, is a personal choice of the followers of that religion. Followers interpret all religious practices variously. There is no religion, including Islam, which is devoid of diversity of practices and opinions. Within Islamic jurisprudence too there is diversity among followers of different sects. The issue here, however, is that of disrobing or stripping women of any garments they wear with an intent to humiliate them and their community.

In its wisdom the honourable court framed hijab worn by Muslim girl students as a garment inessential to Islam and therefore the courts took it upon themselves to prevent the girls from wearing this garment. Even if we accept the "reformist" logic of the pronouncements of KHC judgement, we can see clearly that it achieves regulation of Islamic garment practices through bans but completely sidesteps the question of access to education. Instead, what this judgment has achieved is to arm the communal

---

4. Verma, Subodh. 'Muslim girls' enrolment in primary schools up 33% against average of 5%.' *The Times of India*, 22 August 2022.http://timesofindia.indiatimes.com/articleshow/15564663.cms.

5. Barman, Sourav Roy. 'Steady upstick in Muslim girls going to schools, colleges'. *The Indian Express*, 13 February 2022.https://indianexpress.com/article/india/steady-uptick-in-muslim-girls-going-to-schools-colleges.

bigoted mindset with impunity to target Muslim women and obstruct their access to public educational institutions in parts of country, especially where BJP governments are in power. Across the world stripping and parading (before lynching) has been a tactic aimed at punishing not only an "errant" individual but to 'teach a lesson' and to humiliate the group they belong to.

This has to be seen as a parallel to caste humiliation involved in caste atrocities. Addressing caste humiliation in India needed the enactment of a law in 1989 which created a special category of offences. Among other things this law makes it an offence if a person not belonging to Scheduled Caste/Scheduled Tribe (SC/ST) 'forcibly removes clothes from the person' of an SC/ST or, 'parades him naked or with painted face or body or commits any similar act which is derogatory to human dignity.' This same law protects SC/ST women from 'assaults or use of force... with intent to dishonour or outrage her modesty.'

Muslim women have no such special protection in law. However, section 354 IPC makes it a special offence to use force or threat of use of force against any woman with an intention to "outrage" her "modesty." While feminists are not enamoured of the term, in 2007, the Supreme Court of India defined "modesty" widely to include many forms of coercion, including 'removing her saree.' The decisive factors in determining culpability, the SC said, were to be the 'intention of the accused' and 'the reaction of the woman.'

Many legal experts said that this reflected the increased sensitivity in law of sexual dignity of women. Indeed, this definition of outraging the modesty, which includes the use of words, sounds, gestures, and exhibiting objects with sexual connotations, can be used to protect the sexual autonomy of women in spaces not falling within harassment at work place.

The problematisation of terms such as "honour" and "virtue" is an important contribution of feminist critique, which has pointed out rightly the use of these concepts to snatch away the agency of women. However, when it comes to garments there has been a liberal feminist confusion on sexual autonomy being inherently present or absent from particular garments.[6] This leads them to fixate against one garment and miss out that all clothing is about the contextual politics of covering/nakedness and has been deployed often enough in history to empower or humiliate communities. Broadly the liberal view has shown a tendency to share with Hindutva an essentialised view of Muslims. This is in line with the tendency of liberal feminist discourse to aid neo-liberal and neo-imperialist agendas which are also often Islamophobic in content and approach globally. Not just on sartorial choices but on several other important matters such as the debate on Uniform Civil Code, liberal feminists have held stereotypical and Islamophobic conceptions of Muslim women.

---

6. Chakravarty, Ipsita, 'On a feminist Twitter handle, liberals debate whether the niqab is oppressive'. *Scroll*, 27 July 2015.https://scroll.in/article/737015/on-a-feminist-twitter-handle-liberals-debate-whether-the-niqab-is-oppressive. Gogoi, Surajand Angshuman Choudhary, 'Hijab Ban: How some liberals are sleepwalking into the trap set by Hindu nationalists'. *Scroll*, 17 February2022.https://scroll.in/article/1017559/hijab-ban-how-some-liberals-are-sleepwalking-into-the-trap-set-by-hindutva-nationalists. See examples: Singh, Tavleen, 'Look behind the hijab'. *The Indian Express*, 14 February2022, https://indianexpress.com/article/opinion/columns/tavleen-singh-writes-karnataka-hijab-row-muslim-women-controversy-dress-code. Sagarika Ghose, Twitter Post, February 7, 2022, 4:13 pm, https://twitter.com/sagarikaghose/status. Shabnam Hashmi, Twitter Post, February 8, 2022, 11:40 pm, https://twitter.com/ShabnamHashmi/status.

Add to this confusion the fact that whatever Muslim practice happens to be in the eye of a storm, they are usually deemed undeserving of sympathy. Muslims are always being lectured as recalcitrant pupils who refuse to learn to be progressive or be reasonable. Ergo, 'they need to be taught a lesson,' and disrobing is a classic punishment.

The right wingers seek to teach them a different lesson and but a lot more self-reflexivity is expected from liberal-progressives who wish to teach Muslims "superior" liberal values. Like the earlier mentioned matter of Uniform Civil Code they have to be cognizant of the fact that their knee-jerk, anti-hijab stance unites them with Hindutva groups in blaming the victim.

It has to be pointed out that Muslim women are not the only ones to have challenged the ideas of western liberal feminism. In the West, women of colour including women scholars of Indian origin like Gayatri Chakravorty Spivak and Chandra Mohanty Talpade have challenged this brand of feminism as white women's feminism. Feminism has also been critiqued for its easy co-option by neo-liberal capitalism by many white feminist scholars such as Nancy Fraser. There are many kinds of feminisms, and whether anyone likes the label feminism or not, women's rights advocates agree that their struggle is to ensure that women have autonomy over their bodies, their labour and their intellect. They may disagree with how they should exercise this autonomy and what to do with it. Therefore, the rejection of the hypocrisy in liberal, lean-in, corporate feminism (and the values associated with them) should not be framed like a 'problem of Muslim women.'

Muslim women's voices are not represented in mainstream media and popular culture because the common image perpetuated and popularised through media is that Muslim women are oppressed and therefore cannot have a voice. I have argued in my book *Muslim Women Speak* that it is not true that Muslim women have no voice, the truth is rather that there was no readiness in Indian public sphere to listen to Muslim women and no interest in finding out their opinions and experiences.

It was commonly assumed by even the women's rights activists in India that Muslim women do not understand politics or do not have political opinions. During the Anti-CAA movement, I heard expressions of "pleasant surprise" when the women activists hear Muslim women's sharp articulation. In my reading this expression of surprise might have been a confession of sorts that they had indeed never "heard" Muslim women. However, there was not enough self-reflexivity on this aspect and often explanatory theories were forwarded which rehashed the existing stereotypes about Muslim women. Just as examples, one such theory was of Muslim women being "politicized" by their 'coming out in public spaces.' This implied that the Muslim women's political articulation was a flash, inexplicable phenomenon which almost sounded like magic. This reflected that there was still the insistence that Muslim women had been per-force secluded into ignorance and it was occupying public spaces which had resulted into "emergence" of political understanding. The truth that it was their political critique which led them to occupy public spaces seemed rather hard to accept. Another theory was that these were working class women, which regurgitated the erroneous theory that working class people are inherently more revolutionary and anti-establishment, that only class divisions oppress and that it is class consciousness only which allows people the agency to oppose their oppression.

Through their sharp and unambiguous articulation in the movement Muslim women were able to force the media and public sphere to take notice of their opinions and listen to them. It was this which was unprecedented, and not that Indian Muslim women could speak for themselves.

Muslim women's pushback to Hindutva discourse in the Bulli-bai and Sulli-deals incident and the current debate around Hijab in India is in fact an important moment showing generational shifts in feminist understanding of issues thrown up by time and context, or in other words, history and culture politics.

I take this opportunity to invite a reflection on the history of Indian women rights activists' stance on political representation. In the constituent assembly debates at the founding moments of the republic Indian women rejected the very idea of proportionate representation as being unjust and an affront to their notion of equality. The landmark report of the Committee on the Status of Women in India in 1975 again skirted this issue despite the dissent by Vina Majumdar and Lotika Sarkar.[7] It has been decades today that the demand for 33% reservation in Parliament has been in a state of limbo because of women's movements still evolving when it comes to understanding of caste. On the broader debate on the caste privilege of upper caste feminists this is a very important moment for the feminist/women's rights movement in India. We might remind ourselves how radical feminists across the world have found themselves to

---

7. *Towards equality: Report of the Committee on the Status of Women in India.* Govt. of India, Ministry of Education & Social Welfare, Dept. of Social Welfare, 1974. S. Nurul Hasan, Phulrenu Guha, Maniben Kara, Savitri Shyam Neera, Dogra Vikram Mahajan, Leela Dube, Sakina A. Hasan, Urmila Haksar, Lotika Sarkar and Vina Majumdar were the members of this Committee on the Status of Women in India.

be in the shallow end on the 'transwomen are women too' debate and are being schooled by the younger feminists, another important and hard to learn lesson. Rather than look at it all as a "crisis" we might do well to engage in a deeper feminist praxis.

In the context of Muslim women's rights, the old guard in the civil society and women's movement in India needs urgently to update themselves on emerging and nuanced understanding on civic liberties and cultural rights of minorities. They may consider learning from other movements such as Black Lives Matter. Otherwise, one fails to imagine what it would take for the idea that Muslim women have no agency and a flawed understanding of issues that concern them, to be thrown into the dustbins of feminist thought.

Many women find sari to be an extremely inconvenient garment. Most women who dress for convenience wear a sari only on ceremonial occasions. However, many women wear saris all the time as a garment appropriate to their cultural milieu. Does that qualify as indoctrination? Salwar suit has today become a dress accepted by conservatives all over India, however less than half a century ago it was radical for a married woman in Uttar Pradesh, to wear the "Punjabi suit."

Many Muslim women find burqa a dress of convenience which helps them hide their poverty with dignity. Many young Muslim women adorn expensive, smartly cut and accessorised abayas as a personal fashion statement. For some it is a political statement against global Islamophobia or local communalism, for others wearing a garment is connected to practice of personal religious piety. Many women do not wear hijab or garments since they see it marking a practice of purdah (like ghoonghat), yet they assert the idea of dressing modestly. And yes, many women do feel forced to wear some form of purdah. Many hijabis or those who dress modestly are fiercely autonomous in personal decision-making. On the other hand, many women who wear so-called "modern" garments often cannot exercise autonomy and may even be deeply patriarchal and anti-feminist.

The culture-elites (including Muslims elites)—who claim to speak for Muslims—should realise that their refusal to engage with complex and changing realities and their insistence on the old framing is a kind of orthodoxy, not a higher moral ground. Even as someone finds a garment distasteful, they have no business either disrobing or advocating the disrobing of its wearer, as long as the wearer asserts her right to wear it.

We are all familiar with the history of imperialism and colonialism in which the "saviour complex" of dominant groups gave the cloak of respectability to the oppression of those the self-designated saviours actively labelled as "backward," "primitive," or "fanatic." Resonating this, "saviour" white women or upper caste Hindu women or even liberal Muslim men and women, insist that hijabi women are oppressed and then they force "empowerment" on them. Discussions on socialisation, agency and self-representation will continue to remain difficult and contentious. But we need to be alive and alert to the politics of representation that perpetuates prejudices and takes away autonomy of women.

An anecdote which might show this complexity was shared with me once by a group of documentary filmmakers who made a film on women's access to public spaces a few years ago.

While shooting a sequence of a group of young Muslim women playing football, they noticed that the girls had taken off their scarves before playing. As the game proceeded a photographer from a popular mainstream media daily landed to shoot a few pictures of them. The girls kept playing without a care until the photographer disrupted their game and asked them to put their scarves back on so that he could get a shot of 'Muslim women playing football.' While the young women were slightly irritated at their game being disrupted, they put the scarves back on and passed the ball around for a while so that the photographer got the picture he wanted and not the picture that the young women's activities naturally offered. After the brief photoshoot, the women removed their scarves again and resumed their match.

The filmmakers tell me that these Muslim girl football players now have their own social media presence, where they post photos of themselves and their work as they like asserting their Muslimness as they please and negotiating with the virtual discussions on their own terms.

India has a large private sector in education and the Karnataka High court judgement will of course be disruptive for the education trajectories of the affected girls in the immediate years. However, overall, I do not believe that Muslim girls and their parents will be discouraged enough to give up on their aspirations to get educated. I believe and hope that Muslim communities themselves now might be forced to look for and create alternatives for Muslim girls' education.

References

Barman, Sourav Roy. "Steady upstick in Muslim girls going to schools, colleges." *The Indian Express*, 13 February 2022. https://indianexpress.com/article/india/steady-uptick-in-muslim-girls-going-to-schools-colleges.

Burdukiewicz, Michael J. "The Origin of Symbolic Behavior of Middle Palaeolithic Humans: Recent Controversies." *Quaternary International*, vol. 326-327, 2014. pp. 398–405.

Chakravarty, Ipsita."On a feminist Twitter handle, liberals debate whether the niqab is oppressive." *Scroll*, 27 July 2015. https://scroll.in/article/737015/on-a-feminist-twitter-handle-liberals-debate-whether-the-niqab-is-oppressive.

Ghose, Sagarika. Twitter Post, February 7, 2022, 4:13 pm. https://twitter.com/sagarikaghose/status.

Gilligan, Ian. "Clothing and modern human behaviour: Prehistoric Tasmanic as a case study." *Archaeology in Oceania*, vol. 42, no. 4, 2013, pp. 102-111.

Hasan, Nurul S. et al. *Towards equality: Report of the Committee on the Status of Women in India.*Ministry of Education & Social Welfare, 1974.

Hashmi, Shabnam. Twitter Post, February 8, 2022, 11:40 pm. https://twitter.com/ShabnamHashmi/status.

Rampal, Nikhil. "Muslims' enrolment in higher education rises by 37%, gender parity also improves." *The Print*, 29 July 2018. https://theprint.in/india/governance/muslims-enrolment-in-higher-education-rises-by-37-gender-parity-also-improves/90152/.

Singh, Tavleen. "Look behind the hijab." *The Indian Express*, 14 February 2022. https://indianexpress.com/article/opinion/columns/tavleen-singh-writes-karnataka-hijab-row-muslim-women-controversy-dress-code.

"Hijab Row: Focus back on Sabarimala case pending before SC." *The Times of India*, 16 March2022,https://timesofindia.indiatimes.com/india/hijab-row-focus-back-on-sabarimala-case-pending-before-sc/articleshow/90243976.cms.

Verma, Shubodh. "Muslim girls' enrolment in primary schools up 33% against average of 5%." *The Times of India*, 20 August 2022. http://timesofindia.indiatimes.com/articleshow/15564663.cms.

MUSLIM WOMEN AND HIJAB
Majoritarian Politics and Veiled Resistance in India

Sana Aziz

Tere maathey ka ye aa'nchal bahut hi Khoob hai lekin
Tuu is aa'nchal se ek parcham bana leti to achcha tha
[This veil of your forehead is very good but,
If you would have made a flag from this veil, it would
be better]

This couplet was written by Majaz Lakhnawi (1911-1955)
who was very active when India became independent
followed by partition on religious grounds. These lines from
his famous poem *Naujawan Khatoon se Khitaab* (Addressing
a Young Lady) were composed in pre-Partition India,
to instill the nationalist spirit and fearlessness in women
against the British rule that was increasingly becoming
tyrannical. The British repressed Indian revolutionaries in
all possible ways. In women, he found a great potential
of fighting spirit and fearlessness which were necessary to
make the freedom struggle more impactful. As a poet of
the Progressive Writers' movement he had firm belief in the
secular foundations of India that national leaders of his time

like Gandhi, Ambedkar, Patel, Maulana Azad and others were laying in the form of the constitution. He, like many other poets, rejected the idea of a new Muslim country and continued to instill in people love and faith for India through poetry.

I write this as a woman growing up in an India as imagined by these leaders: sovereign, socialist, secular, democratic Republic. It was resolved to ensure all the citizens *social, economic and political **Justice**, **Liberty** of thought, expression, belief, faith and worship, **Equality** of status, and of opportunity; and to promote among them all **Fraternity** assuring the dignity of the individual and the unity and integrity of the Nation.*[1] It was in this India that I acquired multiple public identities: an Indian citizen, a practicing Muslim, a researcher and a University faculty member. Studying in a convent school and then in the cosmopolitan atmosphere of Delhi University, religious and cultural identities were complex and open for many of us. I chose not to wear the hijab, though many women from my extended family choose to wear it. I faced no resistance, and was never asked to follow them. In the last few decades, hijab has emerged as more than just a piece of garment worn as a religious obligation. It has developed its own political meanings. In the present political situation in India, locating hijab in the larger majoritarian discourse and politics becomes important.

In recent decades, especially after the growing sentiments of Islamophobia throughout the world, female Islamic dress or hijab is seen in the context of human rights violation. For example, in 2003, the issue of whether Muslim girls

---

1. See 'Preamble to the Constitution of India.' *The Constitution of India*. Government of India, Ministry of Law and Justice, reprint 2015, p. 29.

should be allowed to wear a covering over the head while going to public schools was raised and debated in France, a predominantly "secular" country.[2] The issue invoked a series of reactions from around the world, some arguing in favour of and some against the right of Muslim women to wear the hijab in public schools. The western media created an image of an oppressed Muslim woman forcibly made to wear hijab and the western countries—that had often used "gender violence" as one of the reasons for their military intervention in the regions of Muslim-dominated West Asia—trying to rescue the languishing Muslim women. On the contrary, these theories generated counter arguments surrounding women's rights to freedom of religion and freedom to exercise their own will while keeping their access to educational institutions and workplaces intact. Exclusion of women from educational institutions on account of their sartorial choice would further widen the already existing discrimination against women in fields of education and employment restricting their opportunities. Hence, to prevent any woman from wearing hijab in public spaces or private institutions in the absence of any constitutional justification actually leads to serious human rights violation.

Hijab: Meaning and Purpose in Islam

There has been a continually recurring debate about what constitutes the hijab in Islam. It is clearly ordained in the holy Quran for all Muslim women to cover themselves with outer garments when walking out of doors.[3] One of the

---

2. See Asad, Talal. 'French Secularism and the "Islamic Veil Affair".' *The Hedgehog Review*, Spring & Summer, 2006, pp. 93-106.

3. Ahzab, Surah. *The Holy Quran, English Translation of the Meanings and Commentary*, S. 33, V. 59-60, revised and edited by The Presidency of Islamic Researches, IFTA, pp. 1264-1265.

verses asks women to 'draw their head-coverings over their bosoms.'[4] The point of contention is whether it means to completely cover oneself in the all-concealing black garment called an abaya or burqa or the objective is to cover one's nakedness and follow an appropriate and modest "Islamic" dress; a deviation from pre-Islamic "immodest" traditions.[5] To examine the nature and extent of these contentions is beyond the scope of this article.

However, what can be clearly claimed is that the tradition of covering the women folk neither originated with Islam nor was it popularized by its tenets in Arabia. It was an already existing practice and can be traced back to the earliest civilizations in the world. For instance, Assyrian law, during its peak period around 7th century B.C. enjoined the veiling of married women and forbade the veiling of slaves and women of "ill fame."[6] Therefore, the religious scholars claim that the objective was not to restrict the liberty of women, but to protect them from harm and "molestation." Throughout the history of civilizations in the East or in the West, a distinctive public dress, differentiating "modest" from the "immodest" was considered a badge of honour. After the advent of Islam, various types of female Islamic dress (loosely referred to as the hijab) emerged such as jilbab (pl. jalabib) (an outer garment; a long gown covering the whole body or a cloak covering the neck and bosom), khimar (the headscarf) and niqab (face-veil). Majority of the Muslim women choose any of these depending upon the

---

4. Ibid., *The Quran*, S.24, V. 31.

5. See Sardar, Ziauddin. *Mecca: The Sacred City*, Bloomsbury, 2014, pp. 72-73 and 156-157.

6. See Bury, J.B. and Stanley Arthur Cook, *Cambridge Ancient History, Vol. III*. Cambridge UP, 2020, p. 107.

region they live in, the tradition or school of Islamic law (madhhab) they ascribe to and their convenience to carry it. Some practicing Muslim women, however, do not follow any of these styles of hijab which does not make them any lesser Muslim than the hijab-clad woman.

Hijab Controversy in India

Indian Muslim women, amidst recent political developments in the country, are seen negotiating challenging political and social life circumstances, and carving out an autonomous space in different fields. From educational activities to entrepreneurial engagements to justice-based resistances, Muslim women continue to affirm their right to be "heard" and "represented." Their achievements often get overlooked in the larger popular imaginations around Islam as a regressively backward religion and growing global Islamophobia. However, after they became pioneers of various political protests against the CAA-NRC at Shaheen Bagh and other places in India, they have emerged as an active and formidable political group. They have evolved at a time when multiple discourses around religious and caste affiliations, nationalism, human rights and democratic principles are being refashioned in India. Consequently, several instances of them becoming the targets of right wing hatred have started coming to the forefront. Their citizenship is being questioned, patriotic loyalties are challenged, and they are branded as "political agents" whenever they assert their civil and constitutional rights. Now, the right wing forces are reaching an obscene low and are more openly discussing bodily lineaments of the Muslim women, assassinating their character and attacking their sartorial choices.

The instances where Muslim women—especially the ones active in the public sphere—were auctioned online under the titles like *Sulli* deals were extremely demoralizing not only for the Muslim women whose photos were put up for auction but also for other women who aim for self-sufficiency today in India.[7] More recently, the intimidation of Muslim students in a Government College in Karnataka over their choice of wearing hijab has made the question of civil liberties of Muslim women in India even more relevant. Then there were counter agitations involving students wearing saffron and blue shawls and other symbolic clothes and religious flags. These occurrences reflect a larger trend to humiliate Muslim women and to instill the permanency of fear in them, and through them in the whole community itself. There are attempts to discredit and de-legitimize protests by them by regarding them as clones of "Islamic fundamentalists" and Islamic intrusion into "pure" Indian culture. Thus, it becomes very important to invoke the question of gender within the larger frameworks of majoritarianism, communalism and ultra-nationalism, prevalent in India now.

These instances are not casual, localized or reflex occurrences and cannot/should not be understood in isolation. These episodes are symptomatic of the dreadful political circumstances in which the majoritarian forces subjugate minority groups especially when a state moves towards becoming a majoritarian state. These are specimens of protracted hatred, cultivated gradually against the

7. 'Sulli Deals' was an open app that published photographs and personal details of some Muslim women online. See Pandey, Geeta. 'Sulli Deals: The Indian Muslim women up for sale on an app.' *BBC News*, 10 July 2021.

minority groups by the majoritarian right wing groups. The open call for genocide of Muslims at various *Dharma Sansads* that are being regularly organized and insensitive remarks against the minorities in the wake of every election further facilitated the percolation of hatred horizontally.[8] The aggressive display of hatred and power by the male students—deliberately juxtaposing saffron scarves against hijab—against a single Muslim woman student in Karnataka becomes a spectacle of shame for India.

Indian media also portrayed those who wished to wear hijab as victims of religious oppression or family pressure. However, some recent ethnographic and sociological studies have proven that many, if not all, Muslim women in India have varied motives for wearing the hijab. Some wear it as a part of their tradition, some out of pietistic obligations and more recently some have started wearing it as an assertion of their identity. The only agency involved in their wearing of hijab is an internal one and that is their own personal will. Their decision to wear it out of their choice and their refusal to demand any sort of liberation from external agencies like the state and the media, makes them even more dangerous to the Hindutva's imagination of India. The independent act of Muslim women wearing hijab makes them appear more fanatical and a formidable threat to Hindutva's plans of imposing a common national identity throughout the country.

Amidst the ongoing hijab controversy, the Karnataka High Court passed a judgment declaring that wearing hijab is not an essential religious practice of Islam and alongside it also upheld the state government's order to adhere to

8. Jaiswal, Sheo. 'Seers slam hate speech at Haridwar Dharma Sansad.' *The Times of India*, 30 December, 2021.

uniforms in educational institutions. A bench of three judges rejected the plea that the ban on wearing hijab in educational institutions violates rights guaranteed by the Constitution under Article 14 (Right to Equality), Article 15 (No Discrimination over Faith), Article 19 (Freedom of Speech and Expression), Article 21 (Protection of Life and Personal Liberty) and Article 25 (Freedom of Religion).

Practical implications and examples from the Islamic countries were invoked for such an examination in the court. The variation in the legislation regarding the practice of hijab in countries like Saudi Arabia where it is an essential practice, countries like India, Pakistan, Malaysia and Indonesia where it is an optional practice and countries like Azerbaijan and Tunisia where it is banned were discussed as well. Consequently, the fact that emerges out of these discussions is that there is no unanimous agreement or legislation on whether the practice of hijab is divinely ordained or not. The question arises whether any court of law can/ should be made an authority over Islamic legal matters especially in the absence of any concrete legislation on the matter in the religious scriptures. What Karnataka High Court adjudicated in this regard was that it rejected one interpretation in favour of another. However, if a woman wants to wear hijab for herself, and considers the act to be an act of personal piety then naturally hijab becomes a part of her conscience and personality. In such a situation, as long as the practice is followed in good faith by the followers and poses no danger to others, it depicts their conviction and their faith. Indian constitution guarantees protection of their faith and allows freedom to them to practice their faith without any discrimination.

The supporters of the ban on hijab in public schools

both in France and in India used the argument of them being "secular" institutions and thus there should be no or restricted display of religiosity or religious symbols in these institutions. In France the question of banning hijab arose because the state of France, after recommendations from the Stasi commission report, considered the practice of hijab as an essential practice in Islam.[9] Majority of the French intellectuals and politicians believed that the open display of religious symbols—in this case hijab—would be a threat to the secular character of the Republic of France. Ironically, in India, Karnataka High Court banned hijab because they did not consider it as an essential practice in Islam and therefore needless to be practiced in public institutions. These instances are also synecdoche examples of how the idea of "secularism" is different in theory and application in the western countries and in India. In European countries, the idea of secularism and the process of secularization had remained intrinsic to the project of modernity, leading to complete separation of religion from the state. In India where historically religions had been a strategic part of the civil society, they remained intrinsic to society and politics in the post-colonial period as well. India's secularism lies in its pluralism and tolerance of each other's religious practices and rituals. In India, we witness a co-existence of religion and secular discourses: parallel and indifferent to each other, not conversing with each other.

---

9. See Asad, Talal, 'French Secularism and the "Islamic Veil Affair".' *The Hedgehog Review*, Spring & Summer, 2006, pp. 93-106.

Problem of Minorities in India

The controversy of hijab in India should not be seen in isolation instead it should be studied in the context of rising majoritarian politics in India. India, withstanding a long history of imperialism, turned out to be a conglomeration of religions, ethnicities and languages. India, has always presented to the world a scene of religious plurality where Hindus, Muslims, Jains, Sikhs, Buddhists, Jews, Christians have co-existed strengthening the processes of acculturation, assimilation, and syncretism. This strong foundation of India belies the narrative that India can ever be a mono-religious or mono-lingual country.

However, as Talal Asad points out 'even if religious beliefs are not coerced in a modern nation-state some religious identities appear to be more at home in a given nation-state than others are.'[10] Mahmood Mamdani elaborately explains this in his new book in the context of genocidal violence in Myanmar in the recent past and tries to locate instances of such violence within the very framework of "nation-state."[11] According to him, the very idea of a "nation-state" demands a unifying thread and the conflicts therein arise as to who belongs and who does not belong to the nation-state. There the conflict also arises as to who should live and govern and who should be dominant—politically, economically, and socially—in the nation. Moreover, we could also not completely detach from the colonial construction of Indian society into two binaries: colonizers and the natives.

---

10. See Asad, Talal. '"Religion and Politics": An Introduction.' *Social Research*, vol. 59, no. 1, Spring 1992, pp. 3-16.

11. See Mamdani, Mamdani, *Neither Settler nor Native: The Making and Unmaking of Permanent Minorities*, Harvard UP, 2020, pp. 1-37.

The only thing that changed is that in the post-colonial period, the division was demarcated between national majorities and national minorities. National majorities are portrayed as primordial and perennial people of the land, who have infinitely existed here whereas the minorities are portrayed as immigrants. Therefore the culture and religion of the majority gradually translate to become the identity of the state. In this framework, the presence of minorities who are not considered as "true" members of the nation-state, in fact they are presumed to be foreigners, attackers, trouble-makers, "others" and not natives. Hence their religion, culture, sartorial practices, food habits, rituals are not considered to be a part of a unified and homogenous nation-state. They are portrayed as threats to the national majority and hence become easy targets for national collective anger, hatred, violence and discrimination. According to Dipankar Gupta, the majority population believes that their nation-state is being held to ransom by religious minorities in India (especially Sikhs and Muslims) and hence they believe that they are the only ones upholding India while other communities despite being given constitutional protection and guarantees try to break India.[12]

The persistence of tensions between the minority groups (in this case Muslim community) with the changing ruling regimes has been a constant feature of post-colonial India. As the larger political narrative of India shifted from secular and socialist issues to more radical issues, these minority groups were subjected to further political, social and economic alienation. The very presence of such groups

---

12. See Gupta, Dipankar. 'Communalism and Fundamentalism: Some Notes on the Nature of Ethnic Politics in India.' *Economic and Political Weekly*, March 1991, p. 573.

becomes an obstacle in the implementation of their idea of a "unified" state—unity of religion, culture and language. The canons of right wing ideology, thus, disregard the very existence of any culture that possesses the sensitivity to celebrate the "other."

One would find ample examples in world history as well—both during conservative monarchies as well as fascist/authoritarian regimes in the modern world—where minority groups had to face dislocation from homelands, lose property and lose sense of belonging to a particular place because of the inability to prove their loyalty to the ruling regimes. For example, in the later part of the sixteenth century, *Moriscos* (Spanish Muslims converted to Catholicism after Spain banned the open practice of Islam) were not trusted by the Spanish state and hence were systematically eliminated. First, by subtle attempts of genocide and then a law passed in favour of deportation resulting in the formation of the first racist state in Europe.[13] However, by the middle of the nineteenth century, when the new political order of the world was being formed, marked by the ideas of democracy and socialist sentiments, direct physical and violent genocides and exterminations took subtler and newer forms of indirect persecutions. But the open genocide inflicted on the Jews for the cause of ethnic cleansing by the Nazi forces in Germany is a well-known historical occurrence of the twentieth century modern world.

In India, the cultural project of majoritarian political order is to create a homogenous society, by transforming or by denigrating existing pluralistic structures of society. Minority groups are hence required to fit into and adapt

---

13. See Asad, Talal. *Formations of the Secular: Christianity, Islam, Modernity*, Stanford UP, 2003.

to the new social order of the right wing hegemony. The communally volatile atmosphere produced in India in recent years as a result of majoritarian assertion and propagated as a result of 'managed electronic and social media' was also simultaneously producing community "heroes": hyper-masculine, aggressive and violent. These heroes now required villains to be counterpoised against them so that these heroes could garner some chivalrous validity. The most convenient thing in this already vulnerable situation was to pick villains from the "other" community and present them as their inherent enemy. At another level, the spread of puritanical religious content of each community was instilling in people a "newer" sense of religious selfhood and the threat to it by the presence of the "other" community. In the above scheme of things, targeting women from the "other" community, which they presume to be an already vulnerable social category, gives these forces a sense of double gratification. Along with the fulfillment of their male super-ego it also facilitates the widening of the antagonisms between the two communities.

Indian Muslim Women—A New Formidable Threat

Analysing the Hindutva ecosystem—predominantly a man's world—shows that creating a "religious other" and a "gendered other" are the fundamental acts through which it functions. Likewise, it demands obedience and submission from the "others," specifically the women. The refusal of the new generation of Indian Muslim women to fit into their category of "other" and submit to any majoritarian pressure makes them a formidable force to deal with. Their endeavour to achieve economic independence and assert their identity while enjoying civil liberties guaranteed by the constitution threatens the right wing forces. Hence, auctioning them online through bogus apps or denying them the right to admission in their educational institutions because of their sartorial choices can only be subtle ways of persecution.

Here one needs to also understand that this image of an empowered Muslim woman has emerged after their long struggle within their own community and with the outside world. Life experiences for them are torn between the hostilities prevalent within their community and their everyday encounters with the outside world. This "new" Muslim woman is not meek and passive instead she is an active and politically aware citizen. Various factors have contributed in empowering them: Reservation in educational institutions for the Muslim OBCs and Right to Education Act has greatly contributed in improving their Human Development Index (HDI). This "new" Muslim woman, who does not conform to the conventional stereotype of being oppressed by their community and in need of protection, shatters the delusion of "saviour syndrome" portrayed by the majoritarian state.

To become more active in public life and to further fulfill their professional aspirations they do look up to the constitution of India that allows them to practice their religion while pursuing their education. Hence, when any ruling dispensation tries to deprive them of their right to achieve self-sufficiency by putting a ban on hijab, voicing their resistance becomes their only legit weapon to defend their sense of self-worth. On the contrary, expectations from the present ruling regime that has time and again attempted to appropriate Muslim women for political gains and even passed a law against the practice of Triple Talaq are even higher.

Recently, young women filled with love for India rose in protest breaking the sartorial and behavioural stereotypes attached with their feminine and religious self. Images of female students that emerged from Jamia Milia Islamia and Aligarh Muslim University—mostly hijab clad—standing at the forefront of the protests and shouting slogans fearlessly against CAA and NRC caught the attention of the media. Their struggle is to safeguard the secular character of the constitution of India during times when right-wing fundamentalism has been strategically transformed into various forms of populism that appeal more swiftly to the psyche of a common man.

Is this feminine outburst spontaneous or transient? No. It is a result of built-up dismay over the exclusionist and incongruent policies of the present regime. Though they bore other forms of social and political persecutions over a period of time, silently enduring CAA and NRC and not being allowed to wear hijab went beyond their cognitive capacities. Their resistance also comes from their sensibilities of the natural rights of a citizen of India that this Act challenges. It is an attempt to reclaim their space in the political and educational realms in India—which they always thought belonged to them. Their anxieties also emerge from the experiences of the psychological persecution of their community where their loyalty for India was questioned time and again in the history of independent India. As Antonio Gramsci in *Prison Notebooks* argues, intellectual activity arises from specific socio-economic circumstances.[14] These circumstances yield natural/organic organizers, contemplators, mediators, whom Gramsci label

---

14. Gramsci, Antonio. *Prison Notebooks, Volume I*, edited with an introduction by Joseph A. Buttigieg. Columbia UP, 1992, pp. 3-23.

as organic intellectuals. The new Muslim women in India can be called as "organic intellectuals" that are emerging as a result of their resistance against the majoritarian right wing political order in the country.

In the last four to five decades Muslim women in India struggled to create a space for themselves in the public sphere by striving against the patriarchal norms of their own community. Their internal struggles proved to be impactful as they felt protected by the constitution of India which instilled in them fearlessness to fight against their domestic oppression. Moreover, their mobility from smaller towns to cosmopolitan towns for education exposed to them a world of opportunities and possibilities for expressing their talents and skills. Over a period of time, they have also built intimate networks based on friendship, love, and, above all, humanity; universal emotions defying perimeters of religion, region and caste. Seeing their new world crumbling down from the sheer communalized agenda of the Hindutva forces, shook the long years of their struggle and brought them on the streets.

A similar need to include women in the political struggle was felt during the freedom struggle when nationalist leaders and poets alike appealed to women to come on to the streets to fight against British imperialism. While Gandhiji encouraged women's active participation in the freedom struggle, poets of his time encouraged women to be active actors in national politics. Lines from Salam Machhli Shahri's poem *Dulhan* (The Bride) tell us the expectations of men from their prospective brides in the politically turbulent times. It appeals to women to break the shackles of modesty associated with their existence and become active participants in the rebellion against the tyrant rulers.

Mujhe to hamdam o hamraz chahiye aisi
Jo dast e naaz mein khanjar bhi ho chupaaye huye
Nikal parey sar e maidaan udaa ke aanchal ko
Baghaawaton ka muqaddas nishaan banaye huye
Utha ke haath kahe inquilaab zindabaad!

[I need a partner and a confidante
Who does hide a dagger in her delicate hands,
And goes out at the frontier, shedding her veil
Leaving a sign of devout rebellion,
She raises her hands and hails for revolution!]

Though written in different temporal and political contexts these lines still hold importance and show that the role of Muslim women in shaping the political consciousness should not be underestimated. College and university students pose a graver challenge as they are intellectually equipped to understand the political strategy of the right-wing ideologues where basket categories such as "nationalism" and "mythical history" are used to create national "heroes" by invoking a glorious past wherein only Hindus were the legitimate citizens of India. In this idea of the nation, women wearing hijab, cannot be legitimate members of the civil society and public institutions. This also undermines how Muslim women have struggled for a long time (with considerable success) within the framework of a constitutional republic, to make its institutions fully open and responsive to their needs as equal citizens. The obscurantist methods of the ruling regime, however, did not appeal to a large mass of educated Muslim women. In response, the young Muslim women resisted, not only to reclaim their constitutional rights, but to reclaim India where they can wear and eat what they like and still have access to public institutions without any fear. Lines from Ali Sardar Jafri's poem

Jawaani echo the ideas and spirit of the young Muslim women that surround us today:

> *Haqiqat se meri kyuu'n bekhabar duniya e faani hai*
> *Baghawat mera maslak, mera mazhab naujawaani hai*

[Why is this transitory world ignorant of my reality? Rebellion is my aim, youth is my religion]

HINDUTVA WITH A "FEMINIST" TONGUE

Uniform Vigilantes, Hijab and the Crisis of Indian Secularism

Simi K. Salim

Introduction

'I feel for my Muslim sisters, but they do not seem to feel for themselves,' exclaims BJP leader Uma Bharti on Muslim women's naïve complacency towards burqa and Muslim law (Basu 1993). By feeling for her Muslim sisters and formulating a language of affective attachment and sisterhood, Bharti is able to slip away from the visceral violence instigated while being at the helm of the Ram Janmabhoomi movement and the subsequent events which lead to the demolition of the Babri Masjid. The agility with which the Indian far-right swings between vocabularies of benignity and violence, of feminism and online auctioning of Muslim women[1], unravels distinct patterns through which

---

1. Photographs and personal details of Muslim women, including journalists and activists who were critical of the right-wing regime, were shared and put up on auction in online bidding apps Sulli Deals and Bulli Bai in 2021, and early 2022. The accused were granted bail 'on humanitarian grounds' by Delhi court in March 2022.

the Hindu-right evolved to fit into India's "secular public" while also drawing its ideological impetus from global right-wing movements including that of Italy and Germany.[2]

Hindutva discourses, be it academic columns and editorials which appeared in right-wing publications such as *Organiser* and *Swarajya* and portals including *OpIndia*, after the hijab ban were grounded in the language of liberal feminism, secular nationalism, drew crudely from Islamic feminist movements of Egypt and Afghanistan, the secular hermeneutics of Quran, and even ended up celebrating "lived Islam" as opposed to a monolithic Semitic religion which mandates its women to be veiled. This production of a right-wing discourse drawing from multiple histories—of liberal feminism, secular nationalism or Islamic feminism—and far removed from the historicity of each context and the implications of the same is interesting. Drawing from critical race scholar Liz Fekete (2006), I would argue that the vocabulary of reform, feminism and secularism is ultimately tied to questions of integration of Muslim women into the far-right state apparatus, woven into citizenship and their allegiance to nation state. The failure to integrate, (here by veiling) places Muslim women in a precarious position and the video documentaries of Indian Muslim women shot post 2014 which chronicle the racial slurs and Islamophobic taunts they encountered at schools/colleges for veiling unravels this precarious state.

2. On Hindutva's engagement with the global Right-wing, See Leidvig, Leidig. 'Hindutva as a variant of right-wing extremism, Patterns of Prejudice.' vol. 54, no. 3, 2020, pp. 215-237, DOI: 10.1080/0031322X.2020.175986

'The Feminist Tongue': Right Wing, Muslim Women and the Politics of Equality

A complex network of what sociologist Sara R. Farris (2017) calls as convergence[3] operates in the ability of Hindutva to deploy a feminist language to validate the ban of Muslim women's veil and eventually facilitating a litmus test on the Muslim community on their ability to "integrate" or not with India's secular ethos. Farris coined "Femonationalism" as a complex alliance of certain feminist and right-wing nationalist movements wherein they use the language of gender rights to facilitate anti-Muslim/ Islamophobic agendas. She examines how the functioning of right-wing parties of Netherlands, France and Italy between 2000-2013 in tandem with the state's equality agencies, feminist groups and civic integration programmes were aimed at stigmatizing non-western migrants specifically Muslims as they "fell back" in the benchmarks on equality and gender rights set up by the European state. In her analysis of the election campaigns led by Dutch right-wing politician Geert Wilders and the ideological manifesto of his Party of Freedom, Farris pinpoints how they emerge as a curious mix of nationalist, feminist and neo-liberal recipe which draws on Hobbes, Hegel and Tocqueville. PF Manifesto affixes Islam as antithetical to the liberal lineage of democracy and in its analysis of gendered violence among Muslim immigrants correlates misogyny as integral to Muslim culture while regarding domestic violence in Dutch households as "unpremeditated" (Farris 29-32).

---

3. Here, Farris is referring to the temporal coincidence or convergence between the European nationalist and feminist front in facilitating anti-Islamic agendas and the ability of non-emancipatory political movements to champion emancipatory projects centered on gender equality and gay rights.

Along similar lines, Liz Fekete (2006) put forth the idea of "Enlightenment Fundamentalism" where she talks about the ability of the right-wing to formulate legal and administrative structures to discriminate against Muslims. Here discrimination is legitimized owing to the inability of the Muslim community to integrate to (European) values of liberal democracy and gender rights. Eric Fassin's (2012) proposition of "Sexual Nationalisms" analyzes the European right-wing's ideological rejection of Muslim immigration and eventually citizenship for being a community as always already antithetical to the universal values of liberty and equality. Here, taking a cue from Farris, Fekete and Fassin my reading is anchored by the unlikely "convergence" between feminist language and Hindutva in post-hijab ban right-wing discourses. Evident in the right-wing editorials is the inability of the Muslim community to "reform" (unlike the Hindus) and a lament about how Muslims (mullahs) breach the sacrosanct ethos of secularism, progress and female education for the sake of the social evil called veil (Shenoy 2022). This inability of the Muslim community 'to fit in' to India's progressive-secular cluster is read as their failure to integrate into the nation state which also raises skeptical questions about their citizenship.

Following the Hijab ban in February 2022, an editorial appeared in the right-wing news portal *Swarajya* analyzing how hijab/ burqa is antithetical to the principles of human rights. The rights vocabulary was evoked calling out the educated/modern Muslim women to fight against the veil, which amounted to 'a sartorial piece representing violence' (*Organiser* 2022). Interestingly enough, the article championed a 'Not in My Name Counter Protest' against hijab by educated Muslims. The piece effortlessly co-opted the liberal language of 'Not in My Name' protests[4] as a reform slogan which modern Muslim women were invited to initiate against the regressive practice of veiling. They were to seek models from their counterparts—the Hindu men and women rather than subordinating themselves to the 'diktats of Islamists' (*Organiser* 2022). Patriarchal ideals of Islam, these articles advocated, pushed down the already backward Muslim community 'for their own peril' (*Swarajya* 2022). Hijab was posited as much more than a sartorial piece, a symbol of regressive theological expansion (of Islam) which threated the "secular institutions" and posited a 'hostile challenge to secularism' (*Swarajya* 2022). Here again, Hindutva was synonymous with the secular, for the article claimed, that it was the 'democratic civilized space' of Hindutva that allowed the hijabi Muslim women to protest against the ban. The saffron-clad students (the gate keepers of public institutions during the veil ban) were democratic, resonating with the "inherently democratic" texture of Hindutva for they never raised objection to these Muslim women or their slogans (*Swarajya* 2022).

Similar to debates surrounding the 'triple talaq ban,' the right-wing leaders were quick to co-opt the veil ban with Prime Minister Narendra Modi's initiatives for "women's empowerment" and "accommodation" of women into the Indian military. By embracing reform, they (Muslim women) were 'able to play a role in nation building like their other sisters' (*New Indian Express* 2022). The ban

---

4. Demonstrations and protest marches under the banner of 'Not in My Name' erupted in twelve major Indian cities after the lynching of Junaid Khan by the cow vigilantes in 2017. The march emerged as a rallying cry against rising mob-violence and cow vigilantism in India and brought together India's liberal front including film makers, activists, and academicians.

of veil, BJP leader Tejasvi Surya proclaimed, enabled Muslim girls 'to embrace education and modernity' and to strengthen their "rights" (*ANI* 2022). The Muslim women in these narratives were benign, assimilable subjects as opposed to the theocratic threat posited by the mullahs, All India Muslim Personal Law Board (AIMPLB) and the radical threat of the Islamists. The Hindutva ideal of a modern Muslim woman evident here is that of an abstract, highly individualized subject who is also detached from the community which was earmarked in these narratives as a ghetto of 'patriarchal chains and medieval practices' (*OpIndia* 2022). Distinct from the 'saving the Muslim women from Muslim men' narrative which was central to the Triple Talaq ban, Hindutva pushes for an incorporation of the 'modern Muslim woman' subject (*Organiser* 2022) into the nation state, which again is represented via militaristic metaphors. The benign Muslim women in these accounts echo Paola Bacchetta's (2004) framing of the desirable Muslim women who are complicitous with Hindu men and by whom Hindutva masculinity defines itself.

The Hindutva binary of the assimilable Muslim women subject and the dangerous Muslim men have been explored by Flavia Agnes (2018), Pathak & Rajan (1989), Zoya Hassan (2014), Mahua Sarkar (2008) among many others in the context of Triple Talaq debate and (Hindu) nationalist movements. However, distinct in the post-Hijab ban Hindutva discourse is its strategic advocacy to the progressive Indian Muslim women to formulate a modern Islamic gender discourse based on the feminist tenets of 'agency, equality and dignity' (*Organiser* 2022). Here, Hindutva advocates for an Islamic modernist movement in India drawing from Islamic feminist history and the unveiling movements across the Islamic world. Interestingly, an Organiser article drew reference to the unveiling movement initiated by Egyptian feminist and the founder of Egyptian Feminist Union, Huda Sha'arawi, and the unveiling and the subsequent Islamic modernism initiated in Afghanistan by Queen Soraya Tarzi along with her husband, King Amanullah Khan. Articles in OpIndia drew from the unveiling patterns of Muslim women in Indonesia and Malaysia until the 1990's and chronicled the freedom enjoyed by the Iranian and Saudi women before the oil era as they 'enjoyed the beach sun and surf in modern clothing' (2022).

Hindutva's advocacy for a modernist Islam is in tune with the 'liberal, modern and scientific era' in the Organiser magazine also calls in for a secular Quranic hermeneutics grounded on the syncretic ethos of "lived Islam" (2022) opposed to the all-subsuming identity of monolithic (read radical) Islam which mandates the women to be veiled. The right-wing co-opting of the lingua of lived Islam, syncretic practices and plurality is in tandem with an appeal to the Indian public to follow the French model of tolerant Islam. An article in Swarajya (2021) chronicles the French (Macron) government's stringent mechanisms 'to train Imams,' to shut down places of worship if it goes against the principles of "gender equality" and offer protection to 'moderate community leaders.' The co-option of the modern (read moderate) Indian Muslim, the desirable subject of Hindutva, and a secular hermeneutics of Quran to the nationalistic fold echoes the production of a particular kind of religious subject who is moderate, detached from the community, subscribes to the tenets of Hindutva nation state and its efforts to 'de-radicalise Islam.'

Anthropologist Saba Mahmood has located the liberal

Muslim reformers and their secular hermeneutical project which are in tandem with the dictums of the sacrosanct nation state to produce law abiding, tolerant Muslims. Though Mahmood's argument unfolds in the context of the US state departments post 9/11 war on terror policies to produce tolerant Muslim citizens, it has a striking similarity to the Indian context with Hindutva's constant utterance to reform Islam. In both cases, the language of reform legitimizes and whitewashes violence—be it the US military usurpation and killing of minorities[5] or the genocidal calls for Muslims in India.[6] The reform vocabulary enables the majoritarian right to act as a moral force and justify acts of everyday violence, racism, economic boycott which are then whitewashed in the name of secularism and sovereignty of the nation state.

Hijab and the Schools/Secularism under Threat

Yet another typology employed in the editorials by the Indian Right was to evoke uniformity/uniforms as an ideal of secularism and schools as sacrosanct sanctuaries producing the ideal citizen subjects. The veiled Muslim women hence breached the pillars of uniformity, secularism and eventually ceased to be citizens of the nation state (*Swarajya* 2022, *Organiser* 2022). Hijab affected the principles of 'sanctity, equality and discipline' of the educational institutions as the purpose of education is to nurture 'intelligence, critical thinking, reflection and reform' (Srivastava, 2022). After the

---

5. To see how the language of feminism and reform was used to legitimize the US military intervention in Afghan, refer Hirschkind, Charles and Saba Mahmood. 'Feminism, Taliban and the politics of counter-insurgency'. *Anthropological Quaterly*; Spring 2002.

6. Yasir, Sameer. 'Call for Muslim Genocide in India'. 2021. https://www.genocidewatch.com/single-post/call-for-muslim-genocide-in-india

hijab ban, school uniform was swiftly linked to patriotism and unquestionable allegiance to the nation state. The education minister of Karnataka spoke on the role of uniform in 'instilling patriotic feeling' among students which enabled them realize that they are 'children of the nation' (*The Print*, 2022).

While the government was keen to posit Hijab as a threat to the egalitarian ideals and secular ethos for which the educational institutions for, the Gujarat government announced introduction of the Hindu religious text *Bhagavad Gita* in state-run schools from 2022. Introduction of Bhagavad Gita, as per education minister, was as a part of National Educational Policy and to initiate the study of 'India's glorious past,' "ancient culture" and 'our rich cultural heritage' (*The Wire*, 2022). Hindutva/Hindu religious texts were normatively linked to the secular with Hindu religiosity being cloaked as culture and universal ideal. What becomes evident is the crisis of Indian secularism and the evolved meaning of Hindutva which is postulated as the "new Secular" and which in turn has the potency to determine the gradations of equality and secularism to be practiced. Secularism in the wake of the hijab ban and the introduction of *Bhagavad Gita* has evolved into a fervent nationalist ideal with dictatorial traits.

Significant to consider is the shifting meanings of school/ secularism—to draw from historian Joan Wallach Scott (2007)—as carriers of a singular political ideology, and instruments for constructing the nation where every kind of difference was transformed into Oneness. The sight of the Hijabi Muslim women protesting in front of school gates served for the Hindu Right as representative of a nation under threat, the peril of the school which was an indivisible cult, a sacred space for which secularism was 'un meta-ideal humain' (Scott 2007). By the banning of the hijab and positing the veil as the singular threat to nationalistic ideals of secularism, equality and uniformity for which Indian schools stood for, the Hindu Right was able to shrewdly evade Islamophobic taunts, religious discrimination and structural violence the students from minority community encountered at schools. Nazia Erum's *Mothering a Muslim* (2017) chronicles narratives of everyday violence Muslim students faced at elite educational institutions across 12 Indian cities. Erum talks about visible and violent segregational patterns under operation that included separate classrooms, distinct seating arrangements for Muslims and linguistic discrimination. This escalated post-2014 elections, Erum says, with Muslim students being called "Pakistani" or referred to with taunts: 'Don't mess with him; he will bomb your house' (Erum 2017). Added to the apartheid of veiled women in the name of secularism is the strikingly low attendance ratio of Muslim girls as compared to their Hindu counterparts at educational institutions across the country. For instance, in Uttar Pradesh, as opposed to 81% Hindu girls, only 63.2% of Muslim girls attended the schools (Varghese & Vignesh Radhakrishnan 2022).

In the Name of Secularism: Hijab and the Precarious Muslim Women

The documentary *In the Name of Secularism* chronicles interviews with Muslim women who have been discriminated against, and eventually dismissed from classrooms across Kerala for wearing the hijab. Abuse ranged from racist taunts, calling them devils and potential terrorists. Hijabi women recalled instances of being segregated in classrooms,

from school assemblies, apart from facing physical attacks—
with their arms being forcefully twisted or hijab forcefully
removed from their heads, resulting in injuries. 'They say
all of this was done for unity' narrates Fathima, a native
of Ernakulam district, Kerala. This claim for unity from the
school officials was repeated in the narratives of Muslim
women from Udupi who were barred from educational
institutes in February 2022. *Eye of a Storm* documents
narratives of discrimination with snippets from Muslim
women who were abused by college authorities 'for putting
up a dress code that matches terrorists.' These students were
prevented from speaking the local language in classrooms,
apart from facing taunts every day, and a reduction in their
internal marks. A lecturer asked me, 'Why is it so important
for you to wear a hijab? Do you wear a hijab while bathing?'
says Aliya Assadi of Government P.U. College, Karnataka
who was suspended from classrooms for wearing a hijab. As
the women refuse to abide with rules regarding uniformity
and secularism set by Hindutva codes, the vocabulary of
the Right as evident in these narratives shifts hastily from
the patronizing lexicons of reform/feminism/rights to that
of racial abuse, sexually promiscuous remarks, and visceral
violence involving forced ghettoization and eventual casting
out of Muslim women from educational institutions.

The Muslim woman who veils ceases to be the benign
assimilable subject of Hindutva. She ceases to partake in the
Islamic gender discourse and pre-set language of feminism
devised by the Far-right which regards patriarchy as a
solely Islamic phenomenon. This refusal to abide by the
feminist lingua of the Right makes her un-integrable to the
nation state and pushes her to a precarious state in par
with the Muslim male. The image of the dangerous Muslim

women who veils (unlike the modern unveiled Muslim) was symptomatic of radical Islam (*Organiser* 2022) and was pointers at Islamic usurpation of India's public space (Shenoy 2022) similar to Talibanisation of Afghanistan (*Swarajya* 2022). The Far-right "forsakes" its language of liberal feminism and secularism and expresses its "legitimate anger" (Jaffrelot 2019) at Muslim women's refusal to assimilate into the nation state. Here, right-wing vocabulary shifts from that of 'the misguided Muslim girls' who are taunted by the regressive practice of mullahs (and hence to be saved) to being 'members of a terrorist organization,' wherein they proved that they are "anti-nationals" with utter 'disregard for the constitution' (*The Print* 2022).

Concluding Remarks

By tracing Hindutva's dexterous deployment of emancipatory lexicons of feminism, rights and reform to justify outcasting of minority women from public institutions and hence posit a litmus test to the Muslim community, I have attempted to read how the Right co-opts liberal vocabulary to their own non-emancipatory, sectarian agendas. Moving away from its normative violent vocabulary, the Indian right has also made a case for Islamic gender discourse, and secular hermeneutics grounded on Islamic modernism. The evolving meaning of Indian secularism dictated and coopted by the Hindu-right legitimizes the majority as a moral force, normalizes everyday violence against minorities and enables the shift of Hindutva vocabulary, from liberal to vicious, with ease. The hijab ban hence becomes a moment of crisis, a symbolic gesture to posture the Muslim minority as un-integrable to the sacrosanct nation state which is built on the principles of secularism, equality and gender justice.

References

Agnes, Flavia. "The Politics behind Criminalising Triple Talaq." *Economic and Political Weekly*, vol. 53, no. 1. 2018.

ANI. 'Tejasvi Surya terms K'taka HC verdict on HC important step towards strengthening rights of Muslim girls'. 2022. https://www.aninews.in/news/national/politics/tejasvi-surya-terms-ktaka-hc-verdict-on-hc-important-step-towards-strengthening-rights-of-muslim-girls20220315150131/

Bacchetta, Paola. *Gender in the Hindu Nation*. Women unlimited, 2004.

Basu, Amrita. "Feminism Inverted: The Real Women and gendered imagery of Hindu nationalism." *Bulletin of Concerned Asian Scholars*, vol. 25, no. 4, 1993, pp. 25-37.

Erum, Nazia. *Mothering a Muslim*. Juggernaut Books, 2017.

Abdulla, Shaheen. Director. "Eye of a Storm." Strive UK, 2022. *Youtube*, https://www.youtube.com/watch?v=or3McgHl6OE

Farris, Sara R. *In the Name of Women's Rights: The Rise of Femonationalism*. Duke UP, 2017.

Fassin, Eric. "Sexual Democracy and the New Racialization of Europe." *Journal of Civil Society*, vol. 8, no. 3, 2012, pp. 285-288.

Fekete, Liz. "Enlightened fundamentalism? Immigration, feminism and the Right." *Race & Class*, vol. 48, no. 2, 2006, pp. 1-22.

Hasan, Zoya. *Democracy And The Crisis of Inequality*. Primus Books. 2014. "In the name of Secularism: Girls Islamic Organisation", 2014. *Youtube*, https://www.youtube.com/watch?v=slpMrfbGYow

Jaffrelot, Christopher. "A De Facto Ethnic Democracy? Obliterating and Targeting the Other, Hindu Vigilantes, and the Ethno-State." *Majoritarian State: How Hindu Nationalism Is Changing India*, edited by Chatterji, Angana, et al. Hurst & Company, 2019.

Kumar, Pranay. "Hijab Row- Secular Double Standards." 2022. https://organiser.org/2022/02/28/72962/bharat/hijab-row-secular-double-standards/

Mahmood, Saba. 2006. "Secularism, Hermeneutics and Empire: The Politics of Islamic Reformation." *Public Culture*, vol. 18, no. 2, 2006, pp. 323-347.

New Indian Express. 'Hope attempts to push Muslim women into four walls of house fail, says Kerala Guv welcoming Hijab verdict'. 2022 https://www.newindianexpress.com/nation/2022/

mar/15/hope-attempts-to-push-muslim-women-into-four-walls-of-house-fail-says-kerala-guv-welcoming-hijab-ve-2430399.html

OpIndia. "Are Hindus wasting time on the Hijab row? Here is a better use of our time". 2022. https://www.opindia.com/2022/02/karnataka-hijab-controversy-hindus-wasting-time/

Organiser. "Where Is "Not in My Name" Counter-protest Against hijab by Muslim Women?". 2022. https://organiser.org/2022/02/19/73373/bharat/where-is-not-in-my-name-counter-protest-against-hijab-by-muslim-women/

Pathak, Z. and Rajan, R. S. "Shahbano". signs. *Journal of Women in Culture and Society*, vol. 14, no. 3, 1989, pp. 558–582.

Sarkar, Mahua. *Visible Histories, Invisible Women: Producing Muslim Womanhood in Late Colonial Bengal*. Duke UP, 2008.

Scott, Joan Wallach. *The Politics of the Veil*. Princeton UP, 2007.

Shenoy, Govind Raj. "Hijab Empowering Mullahs, Not Women." 2022. https://organiser.org/2022/02/15/73518/bharat/hijab-empowering-mullahs-not-women/

Srivastava, S.K. "Hijab controversy: Time to reflect." 2022. https://www.dailypioneer.com/2022/columnists/hijab-controversy—time-to-reflect.html

Swarajya Staff. "Pushback Against "Islamophobia" Narrative: How New Law In France Prevents Islamists From Accusing State Of Racism And Claim Victimhood." 2021. https://swarajyamag.com/news-brief/pushback-against-islamophobia-narrative-how-new-law-in-france-prevents-islamists-from-accusing-state-of-racism-and-claim-victimhood

Swarajya. "Hijab: Symbol of Pluralism or Anti-Secular Aggression?" 2022. https://swarajyamag.com/ideas/hijab-symbol-of-pluralism-or-anti-secular-aggression

The Print. "College panelist brands petitioner-Muslim girls in Karnataka as members of terror outfit." 2022. https://theprint.in/india/college-panelist-brands-petitioner-muslim-girls-in-karnataka-as-members-of-terror-outfit/876589/

The Wire. "Bhagavad Gita in Schools: Rote Learning of Illiberal Theological Text Will Trump Rational Inquiry." 2022. https://thewire.in/education/bhagavad-gita-in-schools-rote-learning-of-illiberal-theological-text-will-trump-rational-inquiry

Varghese, Rebecca Rose and Vignesh Radhakrishnan. "Hijab row: Why the ban is a double blow to Muslim girl students." 2022. https://www.thehindu.com/data/data-hijab-row-why-the-ban-is-a-double-blow-for-muslim-girl students/article65066546.ece

PERMISSION TO ESSENTIALIZE?

Temporality and the Discursive Production of
the Veil Question in Bangladesh:
A Very Long Preface

Dina M. Siddiqi

Sometime in late February 2022, a friend shared Marieme Hélie-Lucas' 'Open Letter to our Secular *Muslim* Friends in India' on a WhatsApp group (https://sabrangindia.in/article/open-letter-our-secular-muslim-friends-india, italics mine). One of the founders of Women Living Under Muslim Laws (WLUML), the French-Algerian evidently felt compelled to speak out in light of the so-called hijab "row" in the southern Indian state of Karnataka, news of which had gone viral internationally.[1] Part rebuke, part cautionary tale, Hélie-Lucas' text called on Muslim activists to guard against creeping Islamization, even as they defended the right of girls in headscarves to access educational institutions. For, in her words, 'the defense of victims of one (majority) religious fundamentalist extreme right should not lead to supporting another (be it minority) one.' One can hardly disagree with

---

1. Arya, Divya. 'Karnataka hijab controversy is polarising its classrooms'. *BBC News*, 16 February 2022. https://www.bbc.com/news/world-asia-india-60384681

this general statement, or at least the sentiment behind it. What bears further scrutiny, however, is the absolute presumption that Muslim extremists pose a lurking future threat, despite assertions to the contrary by Hélie-Lucas' India-based interlocutors. Below, the author gently chides her Indian friends for refusing to recognize the danger in their midst:

'Now the question remains: how to defend the endangered Muslim minority against the new Hinduist extreme right without giving in to the Muslim extreme-right *whose active political presence within the Muslim community you, friends, have refused for so long to acknowledge?*' (Ibid, italics mine.)

Leaving aside the problematic equivalence she makes between majority and minority "fundamentalisms" in the above statement, Hélie-Lucas raises a legitimate concern. How do feminist activists protect the rights of women without becoming complicit in larger right wing political projects? This is a question with which Indian feminists have long grappled in relation to the rise of the Hindu right wing. With respect to the veil question, Hélie-Lucas is unequivocal, and universalizing in her approach:

'One should also firmly refuse to promote women covering either as a religious right (contested unanimously, may I remind you, by all progressive scholars of Islam on different continents, who paid with their lives their political courage and religious integrity), nor as an individual choice.'

The author resorts to what we might call 'the slippery slope argument'—the assumption that the appearance of the headscarf is always a harbinger of extremist and misogynist Islam to come,[2] therefore must be stamped out now, even

---

2. Time is central to cultural anxieties around Muslim women, who

at the cost of disregarding otherwise key liberal democratic principles—namely the individual's right to autonomy and religious freedom. Hélie-Lucas' provocation joins the ongoing, deeply contested, and seemingly intractable debates around Muslim women's right to cover that have consumed feminists in Euro-America and the so-called Muslim world for at least the last two decades. Through her open letter, she aligns herself with what some would call a "secular fundamentalist" position—distinguished by a refusal to countenance the possibility of agency and choice on the part of Muslim women and girls who veil. Given her general politics, this stance does not come as a surprise.

The unsettling aspect of the open letter resides not in its contents but in the timing, in the apparent tone deafness to context and temporality. After all, even a cursory review of the news reveals the extent to which the Indian polity and popular culture have become explicitly anti-Muslim. Aside from pogroms large and small, violence against Muslims appears to be normalized in contemporary India, as evidenced by lynchings of teenage boys and men in broad daylight that are rewarded rather than punished; in elected politicians openly calling for the killing of Muslims without facing consequences; and in the systematic demolition of Muslim residences and businesses in the name of law and order. At least one expert has warned of an impending genocide of Muslim Indians.[3] Absolute abjection, if not complete elimination of an otherwise heterogeneous

---

are invariably 'emplaced and embodied in pre-modern temporalities,' therefore deemed not of secular modern time (Ghumkhor and Pardy 396).

3. 'Expert warns of impending "genocide" of Muslims in India'. Al-Jazeera. 16 January 2022.

population appears to be a major objective of contemporary Hindu majoritarian state and society.

Muslim women have been central to this long-term effort to 'Make India Hindu.'[4] From campaigns against so-called Love Jihad to the online "auctioning" of outspoken professional Muslim women, not to mention horrific rapes and mutilation during the Gujarat pogrom in 2002, Muslim women's bodies have been crucial sites of signification for Hindutva politics. Any attempt to make sense of the current hijab debates must surely be situated within this specific politics and history. Shorn of context and historical specificity, the open letter begs the question—what is the ideological work performed by the identification of Islam as danger to Indian Muslims at this particular political moment?

Framing Islam as the undiagnosed problem and source of future violence at this juncture erases the actual and on-going violence perpetrated by Hindutva forces on Muslims. Aggressors and victims are effectively reversed even as violence on Muslim women is invisibilized. The argument rests on a much-rehearsed yet resilient trope of Muslim men as always potentially violent and Muslim women as victims in need of saving—to be rescued before they are transformed into agents of extremism. This implicit validation of Islamophobia dangerously reinforces the Hindu nationalist position, making right wing analysis and practice appear rational. The production of fear and charge of latent Islamist radicalism also encourages state and social surveillance. Finally, the open call to Muslim secularists to act once more places the burden for upholding "secularism"

---

4. The prescient title of a volume of essays edited by David Ludden in 1996.

on the victims, on an increasingly vilified and disempowered minority that bears the brunt of the Indian polity's open embrace of Hindutva/disavowal of "secular" politics.

Permission to Essentialize?

Feminist comrades and friends on WhatsApp were bemused—at best—by my critique of the Hélie-Lucas piece. The conversation rapidly turned to the situation in Bangladesh—the increasing trend of very young girls in hijab, the fearful state of the minority Hindu population, the patriarchal aspect of all religions (including Hinduism). The specificity of Indian politics and history disappeared, replaced by discussions of the virtues and dangers of veiling, forced or otherwise, in the abstract.

What accounts for this seamless shift in conversation, the blurring of national contexts, the totalization and generalization implied? What kinds of anxieties do they reveal? Certainly, the contested relationship between the nation-state and religion in majority Muslim Bangladesh has undergone considerable transformation since independence. If at an earlier moment the question was whether Islam has a place in the nation, today it is not whether but which form of Islam is most appropriate. The visual landscape of urban and rural Bangladesh has shifted correspondingly, with many more women visible in a variety of coverings, some which of which are clearly not of local origin. Fashion and commerce are entangled in this reconfiguration (see Figure 1). Secular sensibilities cannot but be jarred within this new ethnoscape. Invoking a host of historically mediated fears, veiling becomes a visible sign of Islamist forces not adequately dealt with in the past, that is, during the 1971 war.

Still, why the assumption that the operations of power in one majority Muslim national space can be mapped unproblematically on to another minority Muslim context? Why do temporalities and geographical particularities drop out of the analysis when the subject is Islam/Muslims, so that meanings are always already over-determined? Why are certain socio-political frameworks ascribed the status of universality while others are readily dismissed? How are specific circumstances so easily naturalized and universalized?

Numerous postcolonial and feminist scholars have grappled with versions of the questions raised above, particularly in the post 9/11 period when resuscitated imperial salvation narratives rendered the Afghan woman in blue borkha iconic of Muslim misogyny, a condensed symbol of the dangers of Islam, and the borkha itself as the ultimate sign of unfreedom (Abu Lughod). Along the way, "sharia" itself came to stand for patriarchy in its extreme form. The enlistment of feminism into this 21st century imperial project also promoted a new common-sense view of global women's rights, one that folded neatly into neoliberal capitalist logic (Abu-Lughod). In the new landscape, nations fell on two sides of a civilizational divide—those who supported women's rights/gender equality and those who were anti-women; Muslim countries, at least those with "extreme" interpretations of Islam represented the limit or horizon of patriarchal excess and barbarism.

What is the purchase of the figure of the Muslim woman/girl in a headscarf today, 20 years after the war on/of terror? Among other things, in the intervening years, Muslim women and girls have gone from being seen as imperiled to also potentially imperiling others (Ghumkor

2020). They are objects of fear and puzzlement, as well as of pity. The fears and incomprehension often associated with the figure of the veiled woman tends to be heightened by a sense of urgency, a belief that there is no time for nuance or context in the face of impending Islamization.

Arguably, the new commonsense about Islam and women provides permission to essentialize, to distill a set of key "facts" that are ostensibly applicable across all Muslim contexts, regardless of history, class, or geopolitical location. Curiously—or perhaps tellingly—the mainstreaming of an intersectional lens and rejection of "woman" as a unitary category in scholarship, policy and popular culture takes place around the same time, rendering transparent the Muslim exceptionalism at work. Françoise Vergés argues that French feminist and left preoccupation with veiling and the "Muslim Woman" question in the 1990s allowed contradictions around class, labour, and care work to be side-stepped. In her view, the decontextualized and abstracted appropriation of activist testimonies from the global South allowed European feminists to reposition patriarchy in the Global North as implicitly superior to patriarchies elsewhere, especially in the Muslim world, producing what Vergés calls civilizational feminism. As she notes, critiques of civilizational feminism are often discredited by accusations of defensiveness or misplaced cultural relativism (Vergés 50).

The resulting common sense about "bad" Islam and women's rights surfaced most recently in reactions to the United States Supreme Court decision to reverse Roe versus Wade in late June. On social media and television, analyses of the decision were peppered with references to the Talibanization of US politics and the emergence of an

American Taliban. Liberal Muslims and non-Muslims, in South Asia and elsewhere, participated in this discourse in which bad Islam represent the limit or horizon of women's oppression. One Facebook status lamented that the USA had officially become the United States of Arabia. A cartoon from 2019 came back into circulation on Facebook (Figure 2). Presumably the implication of the cartoon is that the US right wing has learned from the Taliban. Along the same vein, TV host Trevor Noah (who has a global following) declared on his show:

'And isn't it amazing, after all these years of the right screaming about the threats of sharia law, turns out they were just jealous?' (qtd in Al Aqeedi May 9, 2022).

In the above "joke," Noah manages to reverse the direction of power, covering over the logic that weaponizes (the idea of) the sharia as object of fear not just for the right wing but for liberals as well. The figure of the radical Muslim does critical work here. References to "bad" Islam/sharia make sense only if the underlying assumption is that such patriarchal practices and ideologies are exceptional to the US but natural and normal to Islam. Such assumptions obscure both the brutal history of the assault on women's rights in the US by Christian fundamentalist and secular forces alike, long before the existence of the Taliban, and disregard the role of the US in producing the Taliban. The erasure of US history allows patriarchy in the US to be cast as either aberration or the result of contamination by Islam. The irony, as one critic put it, is that, 'There are few things as American as the puritans who fundamentally built the United States. A fair comparison would be between them and today's conservatives, and that should warrant concern. After all, Justice Samuel Alito invoked puritan Sir Matthew

Hale, not Mullah Omar, in his opinion draft' (Al Aqeedi). This 'outsourcing of patriarchy,' as Inderpal Grewal would have it, exceptionalizes the (implicitly white, Christian) United States, even as it racializes patriarchal practices that "naturally" belong elsewhere. As it happens, Islamic law, however defined by its four schools of jurisprudence, is flexible on the matter of abortion, and always puts the life of the mother before that of the unborn child. For that matter, abortion is legal in Saudi Arabia.

Not all instances of generalizing and essentializing need to be so extreme. I recall presenting a paper on Bangladeshi garment workers' attitude toward the right-wing coalition Hefazat i Islam at a conference in a European capital several years ago. Mine was a story about the Islamization of national politics, and discursive contestations over sovereignty. A South Asian historian in the audience responded with a "puzzle" on which he hoped I would shed light: his wife frequently witnessed young students take off their headscarves or borkhas in the bathroom of the elite private university in Dhaka that they attended, covering themselves up only before returning home. I did not see the relevance of this anecdote to my presentation but for my interlocutor, the intimate family resemblance was obvious. Such associations make sense only if the experience and subjectivities of those who veil are assumed to be fixed, frozen in time-space and so always transposable across temporal and spatial contexts.

Vigilance about the constitutive role of context in structuring the frames of reference through which we understand the world and approach intellectual production is critical to avoiding theoretical and political totalization. In this respect, Mary John writes that 'the very nature of ongoing intellectual production could be described as an interplay between *what becomes a problem for thought and what is allowed to go without saying*' (John, 1996, 110, quoted in Lukose 2018, italics mine). When it comes to Muslim women who are veiled, what becomes a problem for thought, and so for theory, is the veiling itself, while politics and history are made to disappear.

The Uneven Travels of the Hijab Ban

The Udipi issue traveled through other transnational circuits within Bangladesh, gaining a prominence not granted within secular feminist circles. On February 10, an outfit called Bangladeshi Islami Mahila Majlish gathered to protest the harassment of hijab wearing students in India (see Figure 3). Their demonstration was reported positively, as a gesture of solidarity from Bangladesh, on an Indian website obviously sympathetic to the girls at the centre of the hijab controversy (https://www.siasat.com/hijab-row-bangladesh-stands-in-solidarity-with-muslim-women-2279139/). The Mahila Majlish's calculated show of cross-border "solidarity," presumably tailored to local politics, raises the question of who speaks for Bangladesh and with what kind of authority.

The following week, Islami Andolan, Bangladesh—a political party which had previously demanded the introduction of blasphemy laws among other things—took out a procession in which India's hijab prohibition featured as the key issue. Amidst placards that protested rising prices of essentials, and called for the social boycott of "munafa khors" or profiteers, the crowd shouted slogans against the Karnataka ban, which it termed a conspiracy. In an eerie echo of scenes in some colleges across the border, some protesters insisted Hindu Bangladeshi women would not be allowed to wear shakha and shindoor until the ban in India was rescinded. This time, a very different Indian news site—one concerned about the apparent genocide of Hindus in Bangladesh—carried the story (https://www.opindia.com/2022/02/islamists-in-bangladesh-threaten-hindus-while-protesting-hijab-ban-in-india/).

Political mobilization of the hijab issue is not limited to the religious right wing however. In mid-April, newspapers reported that 60 women had been denied entry to a handicrafts factory—Yong Jin International—for refusing to take off their hijab. The video of a speech delivered by local labor leader Al Kamran in front the factory premises and posted on his Facebook page, is revealing. Al Kamran's address is to the entire nation or desh bashi, rather than to a limited group of aggrieved workers. The speech first draws attention to bureaucratic and procedural irregularities in the sudden decision to dismiss the 60 workers. Kamran notes the timing of the action—just before Eid. His speech slides between disputes over wages and working conditions—such as the lack of maternity leave and low festival bonuses— and the right to wear a borkha in a Muslim nation. For good measure, Kamran throws around a few inflammatory statements about conspiracies and the temerity of foreigners who insult Islam and still want to conduct business in a Muslim country. He ends by referring to the men and women labouring 'in this sector'[5] as bir joddha or warriors, recalling the 1971 war and the exalted status of freedom fighters in the national imagination.

---

5. Presumably he was referring to the garment sector since handicrafts production, in this case wig-making, hardly constitutes an industry with a recognizable or self-identified labor pool.

Kamran's call for the nation's Muslims and Islamist[6] organizations to join hands with workers in their fight against those who would hurt religious sentiments went unheeded for the most part. No spontaneous movement in the name of Islam and the labouring classes arose, though a number of male garment workers expressed outrage online. In a jab to Islamist organizations, someone named Zahidul Islam remarked, 'Where are those eminences, the ones who were up in arms about India's hijab situation? Don't they see what's happening here?' (collected from Facebook).

This particular "veil affair" ended anti-climatically, with labour and management working out their differences quietly. How might we understand what transpired? What kind of injuries did each side assume to be at stake in this brief standoff?

Evidently, management in this factory did not have a consistent policy toward veiled workers. Reportedly in early April, some women in hijab were paid half their salary, while others were dismissed for refusing to take off their hijab. The hijab-related dismissals seem to have brought to the fore long simmering resentment over low payment for piece-rate production. This then led to collective confrontation later that month. Workers' articulations of their grievances, available in video form on social media, offer some insights on how their subjectivities as Muslim women were folded into their understanding of themselves as workers deserving of rights. In response to a question on why they were protesting, one woman stated:

'We are paid very little. Eid is coming. They've kicked us out. And yet, they keep pulling at our borkhas. Then they give us minimal bonus. We want to join "duty" today. We

---

6. He uses the English word.

came for duty early in the morning. They won't let us in.'

A colleague added: 'We are paid 7,000 a month. We come at 9 am every day. They still don't give us a break. We've worked on many occasions after 5 pm. But we are paid so little. We were told that if we took our borkhas off, then we would get a good wage. If we don't take off our borkhas, we won't get a raise.'

It would seem that the right to cover became the grounds and idiom through which workers articulated other grievances.

At the same time, the veil issue allowed management to obscure a routine practice in the regulation of labour. As Al-Kamran's speech and the above quotes indicate, the timing of the dispute was critical, just before Eid, when much-anticipated annual bonuses are paid. Dismissed workers are not eligible for bonuses. It is not unreasonable to assume that management strategy to trim the workforce before Eid to save on bonus payments—a regular practice in many garment factories—became inseparable from shopfloor struggles over the acceptability of certain kinds of face coverings.

Clearly the meaning of veiling is neither stable nor singular, irreducible to any one reason or aspiration. Indeed, the practice of covering can be read as a sign of the profane in the most literal sense. When asked about the stand-off over the borkha, Mithu Sarkar, whose unveiled wife works at Yong Jin responded, 'Shoitan (satan) lives inside the borkha. The more you veil, the more you're shoitan. You can't imagine the kind of things women are up to behind the borkha.'

Making Time for Context?

In Bangladesh, as elsewhere, Muslim bodies have emerged as constitutive sites of feminist (and other) politics. Bodies marked Muslim, it goes without saying, today carries a peculiar representational burden in Muslim majority and minority spaces. Muslim women's visibility and corporeal practices possess tremendous signifying power; among other things, practices such as veiling are critical to securing or unsettling the lines between secular and religious spaces, civilized and backward nations, progressive and misogynist polities. The narrative logic mobilized to secure such binaries, and 'the fierceness of debates concerning the public bodily expression of religion—in particular Islam—conceals that fact that bodies in present day society are governed, regulated, shaped and represented in many ways, often unrelated, or even in opposition to religion' (Van Den Berg et al. 2017, p. 180, emphasis added). As many scholars have remarked, an excessive focus on religion works to obscure other social anxieties about gendered embodiment and reproduces boundaries between "religious" and "secular" body politics that are inevitably blurred in practice (ibid). Among other things, the regulatory aspects of neoliberal capitalist accumulation—glossed as development and empowerment—are obscured or minimized.

Universalizing border crossing narratives reproduce hegemonic formations, obscuring imperial and national interests, and the constitutive nature of context. In the circumstances, feminist solidarity practices, within the nation or beyond, must be attuned to context and differences in political location among women rather than claiming unity through imagined sameness (see also Tambe and Thayer 2021). This means keeping in mind that power operates asymmetrically and in multiple directions, and that sedimented practices of colonialism are embedded in our knowledge practices (Grewal 2021). As Grewal has recently cautioned, one must be vigilant about the forms that feminism can take since feminism itself is a form of power (ibid). Any gesture of transnational solidarity would do well to keep that in mind.

*I would like to thank Md. Khaled Bin Oli Bhuiyan for his invaluable research assistance, including visiting the field site of Yong Jin international, and Hasan Ashraf for sharing social media links and for his comments on the draft.

References

Abu-Lughod, Lila. *Do Muslim Women Need Saving?* Cambridge UP, 2013.

Al Aqeedi, Rasha. "Overturning Roe v. Wade Doesn't Need Sharia Analogues." *New/Lines Magazine.* 9 May 2022. https://newlinesmag.com/newsletter/overturning-roe-v-wade-doesnt-need-sharia-analogies/

Françoise Vergés. *A Decolonial Feminism.* Pluto Press, 2021.

Ghumkhor, Sahar. *The Psychology of the Veil: The Impossible Body.* Palgrave Macmillan, 2020.

Ghumkhor, Sahar and Pardy, Maree. "Imagining Muslim Women in Secular Humanitarian Time." *Signs*, vol. 46, no. 2, 2021, pp, 387-416.

Al- Jazeera. "Expert warns of impending 'genocide' of Muslims in India." 16 January 2022. https://www.aljazeera.com/news/2022/1/16/expert-warns-of-possible-genocide-against-muslims-in-india.

Grewal, Inderpal. "Rethinking Patriarchy and Corruption: Itineraries of US Academic Feminism and Transnational Analysis." *Transnational Feminist Itineraries: Situating Theory and Activist Practice.* Ashwini Tambe and Millie Thayer. Editors. Duke UP, 2021.

Lukose, Ritty. "Decolonizing Feminism in the #MeToo Era." *The Cambridge Journal of Anthropology*, vol. 36, no. 2, 2018, pp. 34-52.

Ludden, Ludden. *Making India Hindu Religion, Community, and the Politics of Democracy in India.* Oxford UP, 1996.

Tambe, Ashwini and Millie Thayer. Editors. *Transnational Feminist Itineraries: Situating Theory and Activist Practice.* Duke UP, 2021.

Berg, Marieke Van Den et al. "Religion, Gender, and Body Politics." *Religion and Gender,* vol. 7, no. 2, 2017, pp. 180-183.

PART FIVE

STORY

THE COVERED FACE
A Short Story

Noor Zaheer

It was not the first time that the old man had been bashed up. But it was the worst. At seventy plus he just might pop off, worried the nephew. He moaned and seemed to wake up from the deep slumber of the sedative. Faizan sat up and switched on the light. The old man was awake and was staring at him. It was the stare, that arrogant, full of oneself, victorious, unashamed smile that broke Faizan's resolve not to accost the old man on his single point agenda. He had started ranting and raving at him, his anger giving way to bitterness on seeing his smile turn into a smirk.

'Smile away, even though I know that it hurt you, seeing the number of punches and slaps your cheeks have received. Have you no shame? I know I am only a distant relative, yes some thirteen times removed as you have stated often enough. But I am the only one who would stay with you or identify with you. The rest, the near and dear ones have long disowned you. I know you believe that I am here because I need you for providing me money to educate myself and a roof over my head in this university town. But I do care. I am grateful to you for taking me in when everyone else showed me the road to the orphanage. That is why I have never interfered in your lifestyle and have looked after you every time you have been beaten up. But for the life of me I am not able to understand why you have to do this. If you do not have faith in a tradition you have every right to reject it. We live in a democracy. But why do you have to force your belief on others? They have a right to their beliefs as much as you do.'

He must have touched a raw wound because the old man's lost misty eyes were now focused and bright, and he raised his hand. The small movement must have pulled some painful muscle because he winced, then gritting his teeth pointed to the pillows.

Faizan shook his head, 'Don't try to sit up. The doctor said not to.'

'It might be for the last time and since this is about democracy, I must have my way.' A crooked, pain-swallowed smile crossed his face as tried to raise himself. Faizan supported him and arranged the pillows with the other hand. The old man collapsed on them, the small effort draining him of the last of his strength. His eyes motioned Faizan to sit by him, who, though a bit surprised complied, sitting gingerly on the edge of the bed. There never had been much love between them.

'So it is democracy that we are discussing.' The old man whispered.

'I only mentioned it to make my point. There is no need to discuss it.'

'But there is always need to discuss it, especially for me. Democracy, because it is the key to equality.'

'Do you really believe that? You who go to every religious gathering and condemn the speakers. How many times have you been bodily thrown out, beaten up, barred entry and humiliated?'

'I've lost count and I don't really care.'

'Of course you don't. Allah knows what pleasure you get out of being the laughing stock of the town. Must be some kind of masochism. But really don't you ever stop to think even for a minute the ridicule to which you subject your near ones. Oh no! They are irrelevant. You and your mission against the True Faith is what is important and has to continue.'

'I have no mission against the True Faith. I am a devout Muslim.'

'Oh come off it. If really you think that this is for the last time then you might speak the truth. You attend every meeting of the Jamaat [community] you hear of and contradict the speaker. You try to take over the meeting and speak to the audience, especially the women and openly criticize the diktats of Islam. I am told that you would regularly attend the Friday prayers and openly counter the "Khutba", till you were barred entry from every mosque. Religious? When you would interrupt the Imam and blaspheme.'

'Get me a glass of strong coffee and I shall tell you why.'

Faizan jerked out of his bitter ranting. Nobody knew why the easy going, god fearing, paan chewing and hookah smoking, middle of the well to do, landlord from Bareilly, who had come to do his graduation from this Muslim University, suddenly turned into the anti-burqa, militant libber, fighting for the freedom of the Muslim woman they themselves were not keen to obtain. Faizan put the coffee on the nearby table and debated whether to sit on the bed or on the nearby chair.

'You'll have to sit near me because I am not sure my strength would last.' The old man said, reading his mind.

Faizan sat down, not quite sure if he wanted to assuage the curiosity that had irked not just the family and clan but the entire Muslim community of the region.

'I might as well tell and be done with it. This might turn out to be my death bed.'

'I was nineteen when I came to this University Town. There was really no need for me to come. I had finished school three years before and we were fairly well to do landlords with enough landholdings to last us another couple of generations. I was the only son, so there was no need for me to earn my livelihood, the only reason then for educating oneself beyond school. But my sister Hina, had finished middle school and wanted to complete high school. There was no Muslim Girls High School nearby. She was promised to my maternal uncle's son who was studying law in Delhi. The boy wanted an educated wife and that is what clinched matters in her favour. With an assured future in potato farming, I was here studying the finer nuances of Urdu literature and keeping an eye on my sister at Junior College for Muslim Girls.

'No prizes for guessing what I really did. Eyed the girls. Don't look so surprised. I know there wasn't much to see, clad as they were in black from head to toe. But the novelty of seeing so many black covers in one place, trying to see the hands and the feet, the little point of the chin if the veil was lifted to examine a piece of trinket, read a book title. Trying to remember the shape and texture of the hand and the burqa it belonged to, the timber of the voice, cataloging the little differences in the burqas and the laughter, the gait, the slippers that went with it. More than that trying to decipher the shape of the body, the contours, the highs and the lows, the rounds and the curves, making categories, those who would burst into laughter on seeing the boys, those who would merely giggle and make no comment and those who became suddenly silent because that is what they had been taught to do.

'I soon became popular because I always had money, but more because I had a sister that gave me access till the gates of the girls' hostel. Sometimes I would call my sister and she would come out accompanied by a few friends. At others she would see me on the road and call out to me. She would always be with friends and sometimes she would introduce me to a veil. That would be my day. I would carefully memorize the name and the burqa, often holding it out as a bait for a friend who had liked it from a distance. Oh the joy of those small discoveries! Let Newton be the small boy picking pebbles at the sea shore. I was the gallant who was surging deep into the raging sea.

'We were a group of boys who met every evening and wrote verses, commenting on the burqa, sandals, rings on fingers, red colour designs on the palms and the not so often heard voices. Those were the days of slouching at a safe distance near the gates of the girls' hostels, sighing out their names in couplets, writing a message to send through one's sister or cousin and then chickening out at the last moment.

'They were good times and might have continued for a few more years to peter out into the mundane small town life of Bareilly. Then a new member Afzal joined the group. He was from Lucknow and coming from a bigger, modern town, everything in this town was old fashioned and backward for him. Our style of teasing the girls had him in splits. When he had controlled his mirth he asked us if we had progressed beyond sighs and verse. We looked at each other, a little embarrassed because we did not really understand what he meant by "beyond". He lovingly abused us and asked if we had got down to holding any girl's hand, offered to hold her books, asked a girl to meet in the library corner, or smuggled a note into their books. Our red faces must have told him the truth and he shook his head at our lack of manliness. He looked down at all of us but his special target was me. With a sister in the women's hostel it was criminal not to have progressed beyond whistling popular film songs and writing trash couplets. I was appropriately abashed and to make up for my earlier green-horness I became perfectly willing to be tutored.

'Dr. Hussain, the third Vice-Chancellor, had planted innumerable trees around the campus. It was because of him that the virtually dry region of this town looked like an oasis. The cedars, ashok, eucalyptus were now huge trees, providing shade during the day and becoming giant guardians as light dimmed and the dark approached.

'The examinations were coming and students could be found crowding the library or sitting under trees, exchanging notes, holding discussions or trying to persuade professors to give them some extra time. It was harder for the girls. They had to enter the boarding house before dark and at dusk there would always be a rush from libraries and departments to reach the gates in time. There was a thicket of trees on one side of the girls' hostel. The road that led to the gates went round it, but the late comers and the brave ones cut through it to save time. Afzal hinted that the place was an appropriate hiding place for anyone who wanted to stop a girl and exchange a few words without being recognized or getting into trouble. Who knows? There might even be an opportunity to steal a kiss. Think of it! A kiss on untouched, virgin lips. Why the girl would remember you all her life. The first male to have turned the maiden into a woman!

'On the face of it, what he said was just a theoretical explanation of a remote possibility. But all of us knew that it was really a challenge, a dare! For two days none of us did anything. From the third he would give one of us and particularly me a long stare followed by a smirk for no particular reason. Only we knew that he was laughing at us—the cowards! Eunuchs! The country bumpkins who were too spineless to take up a challenge, to accept the dare. It was that silent, hooded, crafty, half-crooked smile that goaded me into action.

'I had nothing to be afraid of. My sister was a good student and haunted the library till the deadline of the hostel. She and a couple of her friends would then rush through the thicket. They would often be the only ones around. The dare was not really difficult. All I had to do was wear dark clothes and wait behind one of the broader trees.

'Blood was racing in my veins, my heart was hammering and my limbs were becoming tense and limp in turns as thoughts of touching a strange woman throbbed through my brain. Two groups had passed and I had not been seen. My camouflage must have been good. Another group was approaching. They were talking loudly, maybe as a precaution to warn any intruders that they were in a group or to overcome their womanly fear of the dark. As they approached, I recognized Hina's voice. I silently thanked her for bringing my prey to me. In case of any problem, she would be my witness. Good, I was on the alert. As they came closer, I saw that they were a group of three, all of them heavily veiled in head to toe Burqas. The black silk burqa with the green lace and delicate red and gold embroidery on the hems was on the extreme left and a step ahead of the other two shabby, faded, plain black ones. I planned quickly. It would be easy to stop the girl in the middle. Hina would see and recognize him but still have the opportunity to run away with the other girl.

'I kept a close watch on the fancy burqa remembering how Hina had begged for it. In the end it was me who had bought the silk for her and later got it embroidered. How angry my father had been. The burqa is meant to hide a woman and make her unobtrusive not attract attention by its exclusive embroidery and reveal her identity. But our mother had been on our side, calling my indulgence a brother's love and blessing both of us. I watched her closely. There was a spring in her walk. She had always been full of beans, so loving, so lively. The other two seemed such dowdies almost like hand maidens walking behind their mistress. I quickly pushed back sibling love and concentrated on the task at hand. They were very close to where I was hiding. As they crossed me I slid out from behind the tree and grabbed the middle one from behind. She gave a sharp scream before I put a hand on her mouth, stuffing the readily available veil into her mouth. The other two ran for their lives. I held the girl tight not so much to embrace her as to hold her still, kiss her and be done with it and then gloat over my conquest. In my hurry to overturn the naqaab [veil] that she was now holding with her teeth, I tore the whole head piece. The sound of the ripping cloth, the fear of discovery, the first kiss coming, everything magnified inside my head and I closed my eyes. Instinctively I had clamped my hand on her mouth to keep her from screaming. I removed my hand only when my lips were close enough to replace it. She had now been successfully silenced though she continued to struggle, pushing, kicking, hindered by her floor length burqa. Her lips were stiff and she was keeping them tight and her teeth clenched. Just as I wanted to let go, sure of having achieved enough to claim success and absolve myself from the tag of being a novice, something between my legs started tightening, almost as if it had an entity, a life, a mind of its own. It grew large as it did just before nightfall. I had always been so ashamed of my lack of control. Maulvi Saheb would give us long lectures on how sinful it was to have a nightfall. Now the shame seemed to give me pleasure, egging on the hands that had begun to roam her body, discovering her softer contours, while the hardness between my legs pushed into her soft flesh as if seeking a way of its own. The surge of desire seemed out of my control now and I began to push her down on the ground. It must have been this that gave that extra bit of energy to the girl and she pulled away her lips with all her might, pushing me with more strength than she could possibly have possessed. She screamed only one word, 'Bhaijaan!'

'It was Hina, now collapsing on the damp ground.

'Somehow I helped her up to her hostel. Everyone knew me and because Hina was almost unconscious, I was allowed to enter the main hall and be with her for sometime. The warden rushed to help her as did the other girls. Her two friends also came, inquisitive about her sudden illness, embarrassed about having run away when I tried to lecture them on female unity. Then they turned on me and told me the truth—seeing that I was in a more aggressive mood than usual, it was they who faced real danger from me. The usual? I had queried. Well, they had been teased by him before and so had Hina. Allah! He had eve teased his own sister! I hung my head in shame. They continued that whenever a girl complained to Hina about me she had always defended me, insisted that I was being influenced by my friends and that I was really a gentleman at heart who had great respect for women.

'But why was she in that old, discolored burqa? One of the girls answered, a little awkwardly. She was from a poor family, had never worn anything of pure silk. She had gone to visit some relatives in town. Hina had loaned her the fancy burqa and had insisted that she keep it on till they reached their rooms.

'That was that then. I came away sorting out what I would say to Hina when I met her the next day. I need not have worried. Next morning Hina was found hanging from the ceiling fan of her room. Even in the throttling pain of the pull and the approaching death she had managed to hold on to the razor blade and slit her wrists. She gave death no option. It is said to be at 120lbs pressure—the walls, ceiling, floor were sprayed with crimson.

'Shame, fear and sorrow gave my mind creativity. I concocted a vague story of her having developed a liking for a boy from a poor and low caste family. Knowing that nothing would come of it she had ended her life. Family honour was saved and everyone who came to know about the incident vowed never to educate their daughters beyond the Holy Koran and bare minimum literacy. She was quickly forgotten. No one has the time to dwell on women.

'I settled down in this town, and after my father's death

slowly disposed off all the property. I refused to get married ... because ... well it has never had any life in it. I have never been a man again if ever I was one before. Sudden shock is said to have this effect. I did not try to get myself cured. Since then I have lived here, mostly alone, sometimes accompanied by a relative like you.

'I have made this town my home because it is one of the centres of Islamic activity. The University is here which means the presence of a lot of young minds to be influenced. It is here that long discourses are held on the meaning of Islam, it is here that women are taught the sins they commit on earth and its retribution in hell. It is here that they are told that not wearing a burqa is the biggest sin they can commit. No man has any respect for a woman who doesn't wear a naqab. Lies are concocted about the punishment in hell, of torture, acid burns and disfiguration. Liberal Muslims who have educated their children in secular public schools, send them here to learn their own culture, the essence of Islam. It is here that a psychological change is brought about in the young impressionable mind that there is only one way to believe—the Islamic way, only one way to live—the Islamic way. The minds are cast into conservative, fundamentalist moulds, where one does not think with logic and reason but fear and dread of the unknown. Many a girl have I seen become terrified of the tortures god has in store just for them. Horrified and cowed down by the lofty explanations of raging fires and burning whips, browbeaten and intimidated into accepting the religious rhetoric as commands from the scriptures, never to be questioned, only to be obeyed. She feels it is their duty, to be ashamed of being a woman. She accepts the naqaab because she is convinced that it is a sin for a woman to show the face given to her by god.

'I know the havoc a covered face can cause. A naughty prank, a childish dare can become a source of a tragedy only because of the naqaab. I see more burqas than I did in my childhood. I know I lose each and every battle. But I also know that the war must go on.'

Notes on the Contributors

Janaki Nair taught Modern History at the Centre for Historical Studies JNU until retirement in January 2020. She was Visiting Professor, Azim Premji University, Bengaluru 2020-22. Her published works include *The Promise of the Metropolis: Bangalore's Twentieth Century* (Oxford India Paperbacks, 2005); *Mysore Modern: Rethinking the Region under Princely Rule* (University of Minnesota Press, 2011); *Miners and Millhands: Work Culture and Politics in Princely Mysore* (Sage, 1998), and *Women and Law in Colonial India* (Kali for Women, 1996). She has published widely in national and international journals, co-edited several books, and is a regular contributor to newspapers and magazines.

Navneet Sharma is faculty at the Department of Education, Central University of Himachal Pradesh. He writes regularly for all the leading Hindi and English dailies on issues and concerns of education for the marginalized, women and policy making.

Harikrishnan Bhaskaran is faculty at the Department of Journalism & Mass Communication, Central University of Himachal Pradesh. His areas of interest are journalism studies, health communication and impact of misinformation. He has written widely on issues and concerns pertaining to the changing journalism practices and its social impact.

Hilal Ahmed is Associate Professor, CSDS, New Delhi. He is the author of *Muslim Political Discourse in Postcolonial India:*

Monuments, Memory, Contestation (Routledge 2014), *Siyasi Muslims: A story of Political Islam in India* (Penguin-Random House, 2019) and *Democratic Accommodations: Minorities in contemporary India* (With Peter R deSouza and Sanjeer Alam, Bloomsbury, 2019), editor of *Companion to Indian Democracy: Resilience, Fragility, Ambivalence* (with Peter R deSouza and Sanjeer Alam, Routledge 2021).

Tanweer Fazal is professor of sociology at the University of Hyderabad. His interests lie in the history and theory of nationalism, minority studies and the study of state practices and collective violence. He is the author of *'Nation-state' and Minority Rights in India: Comparative Perspectives on Muslim and Sikh Identities* (Routledge, 2015), *The Minority Conundrum: Living in Majoritarian Times (ed.)* (Penguin, 2020) and *Minority Nationalisms in South Asia* (ed.) (Routledge 2012).

Dr. Shirin Saeidi is an assistant professor of political science at the University of Arkansas. She is the author of *Women and the Islamic Republic: How Gendered Citizenship Conditions the Iranian State* published in January 2022 by Cambridge University Press.

Shilujas M. is a faculty member of the department of Sociology at Farook College (Autonomous), Kozhikode. Her MPhil thesis from Mahatma Gandhi University is titled 'Dressing-Up the Body: Beyond Covering the Body with Purdah.'

Sweta Dutta is currently pursuing her PhD at Indiana University in Religious Studies.

Preeti Singh is a PhD Research Scholar in the Department of History at the University of Hyderabad in India. Her research interests are culture, gender, history of sexuality and eroticism in Mughal India. Apart from history, she loves to read and write about world cinema and politics. She was a features journalist and sub-editor at *The Sunday Guardian*, Delhi.

J. Devika is a researcher, teacher, and translator at the Centre for Development Studies, Thiruvananthapuram. Her writing has been about the intertwined histories of gender, politics, development, and culture in Malayali society and she brings her training as a historian in making sense of contemporary issues.

Ambarien Alqadar is an award-winning filmmaker and screenwriter. She studied at Jamia Millia Islamia and completed graduate and post graduate degrees in English Literature and Film. She holds an MFA in Film and Media Arts from Temple University and taught at AJK Mass Communication Research Center. Currently she is an Associate Professor at The Rochester Institute of Technology Film and Animation Program, New York.

Noor Zaheer is a writer, theatre director, and researcher, writing in English, Hindi, and Urdu. Winner of several awards, her published works include: *My God is a Woman, Silent Dunes Raging Forests, The Dancing Lama, Denied by Allah, Mere Hisse ki Roshnai, Surkh Karavan ke Hamsafar, Ret Par Khoon, Patthar ke Sainik, Aaj ke Naam, Sayani Diwani, At Home in Enemy Land.*

Ghazala Jamil is Assistant Professor at the Centre for the Study of Law and Governance, JNU. She is the author of *Accumulation by Segregation* (Oxford University Press, 2017) and *Muslim Women Speak* (Sage-Yoda Press, 2018). She has also co-translated (with Faiz Ullah) Intizar Hussain's *Dilli Tha Jiska Naam* as *Once There Was a City Named Dilli* (Yoda Press, 2017). Her latest book is an edited volume on women's rights in India titled *Women in Social Change: Visions, Struggles and Persisting Concerns* (Sage, 2021). Apart from several book chapters and journal articles, her writings have also appeared in *The Wire, Outlook, The Telegraph,* and *The Indian Express.*

Dr. Sana Aziz is an Assistant Professor in the department of history, Aligarh Muslim University. She earned a doctorate from the department of History, University of Delhi and she specializes in medieval Indian history. She has published research papers in edited volumes and peer-reviewed journals like *Economic and Political Weekly*.

Simi K Salim is pursuing her PhD in English Literature from the Department of Humanities and Social Sciences, IIT, Madras. Her research is on South Asian Muslim domesticities and oral narratives with a focus on 20th century Kerala, south India.

Dina M. Siddiqi is Clinical Associate Professor, School of Liberal Studies, New York University. A cultural anthropologist by training, her research joins development studies, transnational feminist theory, and the anthropology of labour and Islam. She has published extensively on the global garment industry, non-state gender justice systems, sexuality and rights, and the cultural politics of Islam and nationalism in Bangladesh. Her publications are available at https://www.researchgate.net/profile/Dina-Siddiqi. Professor Siddiqi sits on the editorial boards of Contemporary South Asia, Dialectical Anthropology, and the Journal of Bangladesh Studies. She frequently collaborates with feminist colleagues at various Bangladeshi human rights organizations—including *Ain o Salish Kendra, Nagorik Uddyog*, and Bangladesh Legal Aid and Services Trust (BLAST).